Contents

4 Communication Skills   51

5 Motivating Others   75

6 Changing Generations   91

7 "Customer" Service   109

Acknowledgments

Since the advent of the first book in the *Games Trainers Play* series some 25 years ago, we have been lucky enough to have seen overall sales of this book and its successors (*More Games, Still More Games*, and others) reach over a million copies. For this, we are indebted to the thousands of friends and colleagues who have attended our workshops and seminars with such groups as the National Speakers Association (NSA), Meeting Professionals International (MPI), and the American Society for Training and Development (ASTD). Coupled with our HRD and HRM audiences across the globe, from A to Z, from old Athens to New Zealand, these audiences have helped us field-test most of the activities and exercises contained in this book.

Also, a note of thanks goes to Emily Carleton, our editor at McGraw-Hill who first approached us several months back asking that we consider still another *Games* book. It was through that request and her subsequent support, enthusiasm, and continuing assistance that this latest book was born.

On a personal note, thanks go to Carol Burnett, another coauthor in this series, for her continuing cheerleading. Finally, a huge debt of gratitude to my son and daughters—Mike, Mary, Karen, and Cathie—who have continually given me their love, support, and incredible friendship, which has made their dad a very proud father indeed!

—*Edward E. Scannell, CMP, CSP*

Through the help of friends and associates with ideas for games and chapters, we would truly like to thank Nicole Engelmann and her associates at Capital Consultants Management Corporation for having such a wonderful company with fun and creative ideas. A special thanks to Gus Vonderheide and Carl Mahnke with Hyatt Hotels & Resorts; Sheri Pizitz; Nancy Barry, the Gen Y expert, for all her suggestions; Hattie Hill for her constant support and endless help; and to the team of hardworking and amazingly dedicated ladies at In Any Event Dallas for all of their support.

It goes without saying how much I truly appreciate the tremendous support from my family, including my husband, Steve; our daughters, Andrea and Lauren, and our son, Jon; and my loving and caring siblings, Rick, Tammy, and Judy, and our parents, Evelyn and Fiack, who are watching over us. I even asked my grandkids, Shaeffer and Sutton Ann, what games they were playing in school to hopefully get some "generational" ideas. So thanks go to both of them.

Writing and research is such an enjoyment and pure pleasure for me, but without all of my friends and family, it loses the fun and purpose. So thanks to all of you for allowing me to constantly ask you questions, bug you for ideas, and capture all your many creative thoughts. And again our sincere thanks to Emily Carleton and Rena Copperman for their help and support and just making it all happen.

—*Colleen A. Rickenbacher, CMP, CSEP, CPC, CTA*

Brain Teaser Guidelines

Materials

PowerPoint slide or a copy of a Brain Teaser handout (provided throughout the book; see Table of Contents) for each attendee, pens or pencils

Time

5 to 10 minutes

Procedure

Create a PowerPoint slide of a Brain Teaser handout or distribute a copy of a Brain Teaser handout to each person in attendance. Tell them that each frame suggests a well-known slogan, phrase, saying, or name. Their task is to decipher the hidden message in each frame. To help get them started, provide one of the answers so they get the general idea of things.

Give participants two or three minutes to work on the quiz individually. Then ask them to pair up with a partner to see how many more they can solve. Allow two or three more minutes for this, then go through the quiz asking the group for their answers. If a response is fairly close to the "right" answer, simply paraphrase their answer to make it the correct one.

Discussion Questions

1. How many did you get right on your own?
2. How many more did you solve when you worked with others?
3. When working with a partner, did you come up with alternate answers?
4. Is it easier getting the answers or making up new ones? Can you give some examples?

1

Using Games and Activities in Your Meetings

Teamwork divides the task and doubles the success.

—Unknown

For those of you who have read some of the other books in the series *(The Big Book of Presentation Games, The Big Book of Team Building Games,* and more), you will find a decidedly different and marked addition to this work.

Although you will still find a number of the exercises and activities that are so much a part of this series, you will also find a volume of content-rich and informative chapters filled with topics and ideas so critical for success in today's work world. *The Big Book of People Skills Games* is a unique work that will serve as a ready reference to enhance one's interpersonal skills both personally and professionally.

In a study conducted by Development Dimensions International (DDI) in 2009, a thousand employees were asked what classes they would like to take to further develop their own personal development. In addition to the expected desire for technical skills, their top listings were "presenting/ selling ideas," "communication," "managing change," "team building," and other relevant interpersonal skills—all of which are included in this book.

The World of Meetings

As a professional in the world of meeting planning, speaking, or training, you are well aware of the importance of face-to-face meetings. While this is not to disparage the use of the virtual meeting, most experienced trainers are of one voice in proclaiming the value of people getting together to share ideas. With that in mind, let's review some of the basics in planning for your next workshop or presentation.

- **Goals.** Most meeting planners acknowledge they don't take time to actually identify the purpose of their respective meetings. Happily, with the current focus on accountability and return on investment (ROI), this lack of planning is changing. In your role as a trainer or speaker, how do you rate? Do you have identified objectives? Do your participants know what they are?

- **Attendees.** For internal or corporate sessions, you likely already know the profile of your participants. For the outside speaker, not so. Here, there is a definite need to find out as much as possible about those attending your program. This can be done through a preprogram questionnaire or sometimes even on the spot.
- **Topic.** What is the theme of the meeting? For workshops and seminars, are the people coming aware of the agenda? Is there a chance for them to suggest additional items or topics to be considered or covered during your training?
- **Outcomes.** Certainly there will be some kind of evaluation or appraisal, but what will happen after the session is concluded? Were there specified goals and what were the desired end results of this meeting?

Traits of Games and Activities

While we recognize that the very nature of the word *games* connotes fun, that analogy is not the whole story. Indeed, if participants (and their supervisors) see your workshops as all fun and games, there may be a rude awakening ahead. The activity can be used most effectively when it enhances or supports and enriches the content of the program. Whether your attendees are primarily auditory, visual, or kinesthetic learners, you can be sure that the proper game or activity will reinforce the style of any learner.

As is true in most of the books in this series, you will see the following traits much in evidence in all the games and activities offered.

1. **Brief in nature.** The exercises presented herein are quick and easy. Time is all too precious to take any more than is absolutely necessary to get your point across. With that in mind, you will find games that range from only a minute or two to some that may take 15 to 20 minutes. While some outdoor team-building events may well take a few hours or more, we strongly believe that "the shorter, the better."
2. **Nonthreatening.** All of these games herein have been field-tested by the authors and their colleagues. Further, they have been used

with different cultures and with participants from entry level to the C-suites.

3. **Flexible.** The best way to use these activities is to initially try them out with friends or family. Check each activity out and then adapt it to befit your particular style and comfort zone.

4. **Low cost.** As you review these activities, you will appreciate that most of these games require very few, if any, outside resources. While some organizations and associations may suggest that copies of handouts be provided, many have joined the sustainability movement; in that spirit, most of these can used with PowerPoint slides.

5. **Generic.** While most of the exercises will show a specific objective or learning point, they are usable for most any group. Your experience and expertise will allow you to target the exercises to the wants and needs of your audience.

The Use—and Misuse—of Games

Recent brain research has confirmed that unless you involve or somehow engage your attendees every five to seven minutes, you will lose them.

- **Preparation.** Do your homework! Check out each exercise's objectives, procedure, and suggested discussion questions. Add to them to make it more tailored to your own presentation style.
- **Brevity.** Make your point and move on. Think about letting the games be the dessert and not the main course. Start with a quick get-acquainted activity, but don't get carried way. For a keynote, consider using two or three activities at most. In a longer workshop, you will want to sprinkle several throughout the day.
- **Purpose.** Be certain that your participants understand why you are using a particular activity and stress that learning takes place during the processing, not the game itself.
- **Fun.** It's certainly okay to be playful, but don't be gimmicky. If the attendees see you as the class clown, they'll think you belong in the circus, not the classroom!

As you use this book, you will find the activities fun and enjoyable, but remember that the bottom line is always "So what?" If you're hearing comments like these via text message or Twitter—"What did I learn?" "What was his point?" "Why did she spend so much time playing that game?"— make sure you always restate the purpose and the debriefing.

- **Don't overdo it.** As mentioned above, the game is always the appetizer or dessert but not the main part of the meal. Use the game at the right time—and only at those times. Don't forget that you don't always need to use a prepared game to get and keep them engaged. Be spontaneous, and even give time for your attendees to show their own creativity.
- **Don't kill time.** There may be a time or two when an activity is used as filler, but even in these rare cases, there must be a point or purpose.

Summary

Today's participants want and need content—ideas and information that will build and develop their own interpersonal relationships. Experiential learning applies to all styles of audiences and can materially assist them in their own personal and professional development.

As you read and review the activities contained in this book, always be looking for ways to make them even better for you and your groups. Don't have what's called "hardening of the categories." Be imaginative, be innovative, and be creative. Find different ways and uses for the ideas presented. Whether you are the most experienced trainer in your company or the "new kid on the block," you will find this book to be a ready reference for those interpersonal skills most needed by all of today's workforce.

Find Your Partner

Materials

M&Ms or other props
(see Variations below)

Time

5 to 10 minutes

Procedure

As attendees register, ask them to pick out one M&M candy. Whatever color they have, they need to move around the room to find the people with the same color candy. After initial introductions, have each group find a partner to find out three to four things about each other. When the meeting is called to order, go around the room and ask attendees to introduce their new friend and share what they've learned about the other person. It could include that person's hometown, the department where he or she works, the number of years with the company, or even information about his or her family or a recent trip or vacation.

Variations

Attendees can instead be instructed to find a partner with:

- The same birth date (or a birth date on the same day but a different month)
- The same astrology sign
- A matching object (can use any other colored candy or other matching objects)

Discussion Questions

1. Were you comfortable moving around the room asking people if they were a match?

2. Did you discover any similarities with this new person?

3. Will you find it easier to meet or introduce new people?

You Would Never Guess

OBJECTIVE
- To have the attendees learn little-known facts about their fellow colleagues, board members, or coworkers in a fun and creative activity.

Materials

PowerPoint slide, copies of the PowerPoint slide in handout form, copies of the list of attendees along with their pictures if possible, prizes for winners (optional)

Time

15 to 20 minutes

Procedure

In advance, collect little-known facts about the attendees and enter them on a PowerPoint slide (see the sample PowerPoint below). Provide copies of a handout of the slide at each person's seat along with a list of the attendees and their pictures, if possible (if everyone is very familiar with one another, then the pictures can be eliminated). Participants will work in teams of three or four to match people in attendance to these little-known facts. Allow enough time for them to review the list and make their matches. This will vary according to the size of the group.

Sample PowerPoint

First week on the job	Has a pet monkey	Dancer in a Michael Jackson video	Was a high school mascot	Appeared on Broadway
Has six children	Travels to Europe each summer	Once a model in *Seventeen* magazine	Eloped to Las Vegas	Met the last three presidents of the United States

Read off the first item to the group and ask for each team's response. After hearing the teams' best guesses for who in the group matches up with each fact, have the correct person stand up and identify him- or herself.

Each team is given a point for each correct answer. Fun awards can be given to the winning team(s).

Variations

If unable to collect information about the attendees in advance, give a 3 × 5 card to each person as he or she enters the room. Have participants write a little-known fact about themselves on the cards and turn them in to the facilitator. These little-known facts will be collected and immediately placed on a PowerPoint slide to be used at the next break or at a specific time in the program.

Discussion Questions

1. Would anyone care to share any other little-known facts that you might have been a little hesitant to state before (for example, that night you spent in jail in Mexico)?
2. Even though you know, or thought you knew, a particular person in the group, did his or her statement surprise you?
3. Was there a person in the room about whom you were absolutely amazed to find out this fact?

Brain Teaser #1

Directions

Work with your team to decipher the hidden meaning of each box.

1.
 	
pösitivē
	2.
	
	Wethire
		3.
		W
		  O
		    R
		      D
			4.
			
			WMADISI

5. CONETME	6. _f_i_l_l_	7. CAJUSTSE	8. ⊘ KLAT
9. speed Internet	10. SIGNALS NASGILS ASGINSL	11. $\frac{\text{SNOOZING}}{\text{9 to 5}}$	12. hEARTBEAT
13. 10AC TITANS	14. $\frac{\text{BRIDGE}}{H_2O}$	15. $1$1DIAL$1$1	16. ni4ni

Brain Teaser #1 Answers

1. Accentuate the positive

2. A bad spell of weather

3. Spread the word

4. Madison, WI

5. Net income

6. Fill in the blanks

7. Just in case

8. No back talk

9. High-speed Internet

10. Mixed signals

11. Sleeping on the job

12. Irregular heartbeat

13. Tennessee Titans

14. Bridge over the water

15. Dialing for dollars

16. An eye for an eye

Why Meetings Fail

OBJECTIVE
- To illustrate the reasons many meetings fail to achieve their best results

Materials
None needed

Time
15 minutes

Procedure

In the "old days," people used to lament the two sure things—death and taxes. Lately, we can add a third item—meetings. Many people regard all three with the same enthusiasm. With that in mind, many meetings fail to achieve their best results. Ask your attendees to form into groups of three or four to identify a recent meeting they attended that may have not been successful. Further discuss some of these reasons and how they can be corrected for a very successful meeting. Time permitting, ask the smaller group to share their ideas with the entire group.

Discussion Questions

1. What are the top two or three reasons meetings fail (e.g., no agenda, improper planning, no goals or expectations)?

2. As an attendee, how can you tell the meeting's facilitator or planner that it is not working?

3. What are your suggestions to make meetings more effective?

Make Meetings Work

Materials
   None needed
Time
   15 to 20 minutes

Procedure

All too often small-group meetings—staff meetings, sales meetings, and so forth—are wasteful of time and talent. Ask the group to think of a recent meeting they attended at their workplace. This could take the form of a departmental meeting, a committee meeting, or any kind of get-together that involved 20 or fewer people.

Divide the group into teams of four or five and have them tell others about a meeting that they recently attended or perhaps even conducted. In retrospect, was that meeting a productive one? Ask them also to discuss what may have gone right or what may have gone wrong. Have them identify the top four or five reasons why meetings fail. Allow 10 minutes for this discussion. Ask an individual from each subgroup to identify his or her findings to the rest of the large group.

Discussion Questions

1. Did some of you have a good feeling about that last meeting?

2. Assuming some meetings failed to hit their target, what were the main culprits?

3. How could these have been rectified?

4. What are some tips for us to ensure that all of our meetings are more productive?

Mini-Meeting

Materials

3 x 5 cards (one set for each team of five to nine people

Time

20 to 25 minutes

Procedure

Prepare a set of 3 × 5 cards, with enough sets so that everyone will have a card. Each card will show one of the following words:

Leader	Know-It-All	Naysayer
Bored	Interrupter	Devil's Advocate
Disruptive	Silent	Attendee

Tell the group that they will be conducting a mock meeting in which they will have a chance to play a role that they might see in their own company or organization. This could take the form of a staff meeting, a board meeting, a committee meeting, a sales meeting, and so forth.

Have them form into teams of five to nine people. Distribute a set of cards to each team facedown, one to each person. If the team is smaller than nine, just make sure each team receives the Leader card. Announce that the topic of the meeting will be chosen by the group leader—or if he or she prefers, it could be picked by the group. A sample topic might be, "Should we hold the annual holiday event this year or donate that money to a local charity?" Have the participants turn over their cards and allow one or two minutes for them to think about how they will play the role on the card they have. Ask them not to divulge their role until after the meeting is over. Allow 10 minutes for their respective meetings. Then have the person who picked the Leader card identify himself or herself.

Discussion Questions

1. How did you select your topic? Did everyone have a chance to suggest one?

2. Did you find your leader maintained control? How?

3. Did some of you get "carried away" with the part you played?

4. Do you see these types (naysayers, bored, and so on) in your own meetings? How would you suggest they be handled?

2

We're in the People Business!

We are not in the coffee business serving people.
We are in the people business serving coffee.

—Howard Schultz, CEO, Starbucks

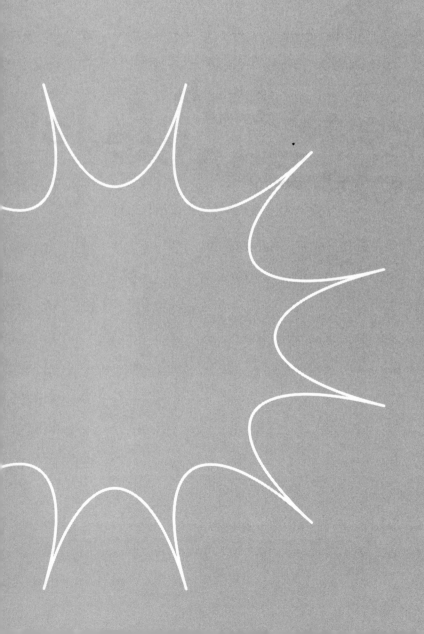

What better way to begin our essay on the importance of people skills than to quote Howard Schultz. The overall success of Starbucks, with all its stores across the globe, underscores the main theme of this chapter. You will quickly see that whether you're in the coffee, communication, or conference business, it's indeed a people activity.

Types of People

It's been said that there are three kinds of people: the type who *makes* things happen, the type who *watches* things happen, and the type who *wonders* what the heck happened in the first place.

It seems that most any organization has its share of all three kinds. The movers and the shakers comprise a good share of any company. These are the ones who can be given a task to accomplish—and then get out of their way! These are the self-motivated people who take pride in their work and derive a great deal of satisfaction from doing so. They come from all sectors of the workforce and, contrary to popular belief, many Gen Xers and Gen Yers comprise a goodly part of this sector.

The second type—those who watch things happen—seemingly are content to sit on the sidelines and simply be an observer to the task at hand. As team members, they seldom take an active part but are perfectly content to let the others carry their share. Obviously, an organization cannot possibly survive in today's competitive marketplace, but sadly many companies find far too many of these individuals on their payrolls. It's safe to characterize these workers as seeing their role as "on-the-job retirement."

Sad as this is, our third type—those who sit on the sidelines but don't have a clue as to what's happening—are a strange lot indeed. One might wonder how they can even hold a job! But make no mistake—they have figured out the "system." This might take the form of walking fast and carrying a yellow pad. Their managers may confuse activity with results. They may appear to be as busy as anyone else, but in the privacy of their cubes or offices, video games or any of the social media they are using may take up an inordinate amount of their workday.

In days of old, we spoke of the "three Rs" of society when "reading, 'riting, and 'rithmetic" were the competencies of the day. Clearly, that is an outdated premise and has been supplanted by the "three Ps"—"people, performance, and productivity." Unless every single member of the team carries his or her load, the firm's bottom line is in jeopardy. And to further emphasize that point, make certain we remind ourselves that without a good "top line," i.e., its human resources, the possibility of a good bottom line is even more difficult.

Positive and Negative People

What a wonderful world it would be if all our colleagues and contacts were bright, positive, fun people. Unfortunately, that may be but a dream in today's society. We see far too many people who seem to take delight in being able to ruin someone else's day. These are the folks who always seem to get up on the wrong side of the bed. These are the type who must have been weaned on a pickle! They're the kind where the room seems to brighten—whenever they leave!

Study after study shows that negativity in the workplace is both destructive and costly. Researchers tell us that this negativity costs the U.S. economy some $300 billion each year. Think about that—that's over $1 billion lost each workday!

On the other hand, it should be part of our responsibility as trainers, facilitators, and speakers to help change that negativity into positivity.

Some years back, there was a popular song called "Ac-Cent-Tchu-Ate the Positive." Granted, this is a very old adage, but its lesson is still very true today. Think about it for a moment—wouldn't your own work situation be a lot more fun (and likely a lot more productive!) if this premise of positivity permeated your organization?

One Gallup study showed that when managers "accentuated the positive" and focused on their people's strengths, more than half (61 percent) of these employees felt far more engaged and thus productive. Further, only 1 percent complained about their jobs, gave their coworkers a bad time, or bad-mouthed the company.

To further make our point, another Gallup study illustrated that those employees who did get positive feedback or regular praise were far more productive, received better satisfaction scores from their customers, and were more likely to stay with their company.

As an aside, a 20-year study at Miami University in Ohio about the aging process found that people with a positive attitude about themselves and life in general actually lived some seven and a half years longer!

Finally, a research project at the University of Pennsylvania showed that people with an air of optimism about themselves were more successful than their negative counterparts in the fields of business, sports, education —and, yes, even politics.

Using this research, a large life insurance company devised a test to differentiate positive and negative prospective new sales personnel. Interestingly, the optimists outsold their negative colleagues by some 20 percent the first year and over 50 percent the second year. Perhaps the positive group had more friends and relatives, but that apparently was not part of the study.

Summary

We could go on, but you get the point.

There is no question that in order to survive in today's competitive economy, it is imperative that companies have a good, solid "bottom line." However, let us point out that without a good "top line"—human resources—there wouldn't be much of a bottom line!

Thus, the theme of this book—as facilitators, meeting planners, speakers, and trainers, our task is dealing with people. Regardless of your title or responsibilities, your success will largely be measured by the way you and your attendees relate and interact with one another. Yes indeed, "we're in the people business!"

4 x 4

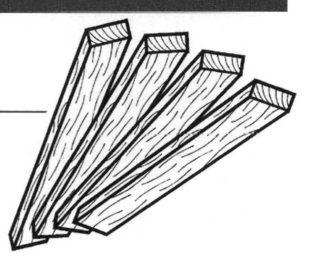

OBJECTIVE

- To make it comfortable for people to mix and mingle by meeting new attendees, colleagues, or peers and to find a common interest

Materials

Clock or stopwatch

Time

15 to 20 minutes

Procedure

Tell the attendees that they have four minutes to form into teams of four. They should work the room quickly, shouting out things they might have in common with others in the room, until their team is gathered. Once the teams have been created, teammates should find three more additional things they have in common.

After their four minutes are up, select a representative from each team to tell their four similarities to the rest of the audience. Other teams can chime in to connect to these same similarities. An example of a list of commonalities among a team might be:

1. Moved from a different state
2. Work in the same department
3. Work on the same floor in the building
4. Started work the same year or same month

To add to the game, have teammates give one another names by adding a descriptor that starts with the same first letter of the person's first name, such as Sassy Shannon, Amiable Andrea, Educated Evelyn, or Busy Beth. Go around the room and have everyone tell some of their similarities. Then have them write their new name on their badges for the rest of the meeting or reception.

Variations

Have participants form into teams of four (or fewer, depending on the size of the group). Teams should identify four things that they have in common that are *not* work- or job-related, such as:

1. Two siblings
2. Married more than 10 years (either with one or combined marriages)
3. Same birth month
4. Same color of eyes

Then each team shouts out some of the things they have in common. The more fun, unusual, or ridiculous the better.

Discussion Questions

1. Did any of you find it difficult or awkward to roam around the room shouting things out?
2. What where some of the out-of-the-ordinary, outlandish items you identified?
3. Why do you suppose you were given the name by your team members?

Six Degrees of Separation

Materials

None needed

Time

10 to 15 minutes

Procedure

As most of us know, it's been shown that almost any one of us could somehow be in direct contact with just about any well-known person in the world. In brief, we likely know someone who in turn knows someone who in turn knows someone quite famous. This could be a politician, a celebrity, or a best-selling author.

While this phenomenon is referred to as "six degrees of separation"—where, within five other contacts, we could be in touch with that famous person—it is believed that with the advent of modern social media, the number could be reduced to five, four, or even three degrees of separation.

Form teams of three or four and announce to the entire group that their task is to see how many intermediate contacts they would need to be in touch with a celebrity of their choice (for example, the president or prime minister of a country or a rock star or TV celebrity).

Discussion Questions

1. How many of you completed the task within the typical "six degrees"?

2. How many did it with only three or four contacts? Tell the group the names or contacts you identified.

3. Since you've proven that this is possible, is there someone you really would like to contact this way?

4. Can you think of other examples in which this activity could be used?

What If . . . ?

Materials

Pieces of paper, pens or pencils

Time

15 to 20 minutes

Procedure

Remind the group of Murphy's Law, which states that whatever can go wrong will go wrong. Let them know that there is a corollary called O'Toole's Law, which states that Murphy was an optimist! With this in mind, tell the group they'll be asked to think of some things that may have—or could have—gone wrong, either at their jobs or in meetings they've attended or orchestrated. For example, some years ago a meeting planner brought in a circus act for her annual conference. Among the animals was an elephant, which actually died in the meeting ballroom!

Ask each person to think of a recent case where indeed something did go wrong. Ask them to write this example on a piece of paper starting with the words *What if,* followed by their problem. For example, "What if the speaker didn't show up for your opening session?" or "What if your boss told you that you had to take her place on a panel tomorrow morning?" When all have done so, collect the papers.

Break your group into teams of four or five. Pick out one of these sheets for each team and ask them how they would handle the scenario described. Allow three to five minutes for their discussion and then ask a representative from each team to read the item and how they would handle it.

Following this, ask the person who wrote the problem how the situation was actually handled.

Discussion Questions

1. How many possible answers did you suggest for your problem?

2. How many of you could relate to the problem you discussed?

3. What were some of the more unusual problems—or answers— you thought of?

4. Can you think of some ways at work you could use this activity?

Take a Card, Any Card (Part 1)

Materials

Participants' business cards

Time

5 to 10 minutes

Procedure

Ask participants to find another person in the group that they do not know (or perhaps don't know very well). Have them exchange business cards and tell the other person something about themselves and their job. Further, ask them to exchange information about what their job responsibilities are and if their job title shown on the card really tells the whole story. Then ask them to tell their partner what their "USP" (unique selling proposition) is and why they are really different—or better—than anyone else doing this kind of work. Switch partners if time allows.

Discussion Questions

1. Did any of you find some things in common?
2. How many of you disclosed things about your job that are not at all defined by your job title?
3. What are some of the more unusual activities you are responsible for?
4. Throw modesty to the winds. Tell us about your respective USP and why you're the best at it.

3

Interpersonal Tool Kit

A positive attitude may not solve all of your problems,
but it will annoy enough people to make it worth the effort.

—Herm Albright

This chapter provides insight into and an overview of all the chapters that follow. There is no question that even in this era of instant worldwide communication and changing technology, the art and skill of dealing with people is still paramount.

Moreover, study after study about why people lose their jobs show that it's typically not due to a lack of technical skills but more often a lack of "people" skills. Obviously, economic times often mandate some of these job losses, but in normal times of business growth and development, it comes down to one's interpersonal skill set.

So let's take a quick look at some of these important "tools" so critical for success in any situation in which we are working with others. Interestingly, even with virtual work situations or in those cases where one's supervisor or manager may be in a different city (or country), these interpersonal skills are still critical for success in any type of organization.

The Tool Kit for Success

As you read through the following "laundry list" of interpersonal skills, please note that these are not listed with any particular order or priority in mind. In addition, one or two of these skills may not even be all that important in your respective job description. However, even in the rare cases where they may not seem applicable or relevant to your situation, it is still important to ensure that we all have at least a good working knowledge of these important skills.

Fair enough? Let's get started!

Communication

In its simplest form, *communication* can be defined as "the mutual exchange of information and understanding." How? "By any effective means." The reason we add those last few words, of course, is to address the ever-increasing impact of nonverbal or body language. Oftentimes, in one-on-one communication, those nonverbals may far outweigh the written or spoken word.

Studies at major universities over the past few decades have illustrated that while most of us spend the majority of our time in some form or phase of communication, we may not be all that good at it. Some research has shown that while the average person spends at least 70 percent of his or her time in communication, it is at about a 30 percent efficiency rate!

Motivating Others

Once again, let's start with a working definition. According to Mr. Webster, we're told that motivation is "that from within, not without, that prompts or incites an action."

Try that again. If you buy that definition, it tells us that all motivation is intrinsic. In other words, you can't motivate anyone to do anything—and here's the most important part—unless they *want* to do it! It's as simple—and yet as difficult—as that.

Take a tip from the popular stage play *My Fair Lady*, which we will discuss further in Chapter 5. If you recall, it illustrates the well-documented Pygmalion effect: essentially, expect the best from others, and more often than not they'll prove you right. By building on individuals' strengths, we help them be "all that they can be." On the other hand, a weakness is really nothing more than an absence of strength. Often an encouraging word, a verbal pat on the back, or some form of recognition for a job well done will materially enhance and strengthen a person and his or her confidence.

"Customer" Service

Note the "customer" being shown in quotation marks. The reason may be obvious. Even if you're not directly serving "customers," likely you are serving someone else who is. And if you think about it, we all have "customers" in one sense or another.

If there is one thing that seems to be lacking in our business world, it unfortunately comes down to customer service—or perhaps more correctly, the lack thereof! Doubtless, as you are reading these very words, you may be thinking of a recent situation, perhaps in a local retail store, where the lack of service—or maybe even disservice—became painfully evident.

The success stories of Disney, Nordstrom, and Southwest Airlines shine as bright lights in an otherwise dim world. The service attitude displayed by these companies and dozens of others shows us that indeed we can all learn lessons from their success.

Leadership

As you will learn in Chapter 10, *leadership* has many different meanings. For example, the late Dr. Peter Drucker once wrote that "the task of leadership is to create an alignment of strengths that make our weaknesses irrelevant." Dr. Warren Bennis, a well-respected author in the field of leadership studies, says simply that "character is the core competency of leadership." One could further opine that leadership is not necessarily what a person "does" but, more to the point, what a person "is."

We'll be taking a detailed look at differentiating the role of leadership versus the role of management. You will see how the role of the manager is seen as directing tasks while the leader works with the people part of the equation.

Perhaps it was true that once the "boss" got respect just because he or she was the boss. However, particularly in the case of Gen Xers and Gen Yers, that is ancient history. Today the manager or supervisor gets respect not by the power of his or her position but rather by the power of his or her performance.

Managing Change

That change is the name of the game is a gross understatement. We have seen more change in the last decade than in the previous four or five.

While most of these changes are from the world of technology, there is still a human element involved.

How could we possibly survive in today's global economy without our cell phones, our BlackBerrys, our iPhones, or the host of other gadgets coming on the market every day? One could muse, as we look at our history books, how anyone could have possibly survived without all these marvels of modern technology.

But back to our basic premise—the constancy of change is all around us. The old saying that "people resist change" may still be somewhat correct, but more important is that fact that people resist *being* changed! However, with adequate lead time and full and open advance communication, this built-in resistance can be considerably lessened.

It is also important to note that our younger generations are not only open to change—they welcome it!

Remember that old mythical radio station, WII-FM (What's In It For Me)? Its premise is as true today as ever—show people what's in it for them and you're already on your way to overcoming resistance.

Team Building

While we're on acronyms, try this on for size: TEAM—Together Everyone Accomplishes More.

You will learn several basic elements necessary for an effective team. And you will not be surprised to see that most of these ingredients are equally important in all our dealings with our colleagues. These include such things as a common goal, clarity of purpose, communication, and consensus, to name but a few.

It is also relevant and important to discuss some of the reasons that teams fail to make their mark. Sadly, these traits often show up in our team members and can easily derail the efforts of others.

In the case of one Fortune 500 company's study of its top 150 managers, the trait of "good team builder" came out as number one.

Presenting and Facilitating Skills

We're not necessarily of the mind-set that everyone needs to have polished presentation skills, but there is no question that as one rises up the levels of leadership, this ability to express oneself in a competent and confident manner is critical indeed.

In a similar vein, the ability to facilitate small groups is an equally important tool.

We are not suggesting that anyone needs to be a top-notch orator, but mastering the basic skills of presenting to an audience—large or small—is critical.

And if butterflies seem to get in your way, you will even learn some techniques to get those butterflies to fly in formation!

Creative Problem Solving

Creativity has been defined in dozens of ways. It has been suggested that creativity dictates finding out how everybody else is doing things—and then doing them differently.

Buckminster Fuller, the creator of the geodesic dome, suggested that "creativity is the miracle of the obvious." The best way to be creative is to just do it!

Believe it or not, we are all creative, but in many cases because of the nature of our work situation, such as a manager who likes things the way they are, we don't always get that chance to show our innovative abilities. We may find ourselves in a rut—doing the same thing in the same way, day after day. For your next presentation or training module that you're conducting, why not try something different?

Summary

This chapter has introduced several of the interpersonal skills that we'll be covering in far more depth. As you read through these, you'll discover that you can easily enhance and develop not only your own interpersonal skills but, perhaps equally important, those of your audiences and attendees as well.

This listing of interpersonal skills offers a "sneak preview" of what you have in store. Unlike other books in this series, you will learn rich and proven content for your own personal and professional development. So as you read through these pages, you will discover numerous tips and techniques to add to your own tool kit.

You're about to embark on a fun and informative journey. Enjoy the ride!

What's in a Name? (Part 1)

Materials

Copies of the What's in a Name (Part 1) handout (provided) or PowerPoint slide, pens or pencils

Time

10 to 15 minutes

Procedure

Copy the provided handout for participants or prepare a PowerPoint slide based on the handout.

Form teams of three or four and tell the group that their job is to check their knowledge of people skills by seeing how many words they can think of to identify an interpersonal skill. Each letter in the term *people skills* can represent a specific tool or skill in the interpersonal arena. For example, the first *p* in *people skills* could be for "presentation skills," then *e* could be for "empowerment," and so forth.

Allow five minutes for this part of the activity and then arbitrarily assign a letter to each team, who will then prepare a three-minute lesson on that particular item.

Discussion Questions

1. How many of you completed the task using all 12 letters?

2. How many of you identified some words not often associated with these skills?

3. What were some of the more common words found?

4. Can you think of other words that are equally if not even more important that no one considered?

What's in a Name? (Part 1)

Directions

In the area of people skills, we all know a number of individual traits or characteristics that exemplify what these interpersonal skills are all about. Your team's task is to fill in the blanks below so that each word you choose is an integral part of your tool kit. Then, be prepared to present a three-minute lesson on one of these items to the other teams.

P _____

E _____

O _____

P _____

L _____

E _____

S _____

K _____

I _____

L _____

L _____

S _____

NOTES

_____

_____

_____

_____

_____

_____

_____

_____

_____

_____

_____

_____

What's in a Name? (Part 2)

Materials

Copies of the What's in a Name (Part 2) handout (provided) or PowerPoint slide, pens or pencils

Time

10 to 15 minutes

Procedure

Copy the provided handout for participants or prepare a Power-Point slide based on the handout.

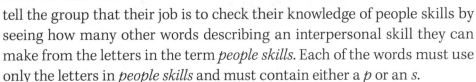

Form teams of three or four and tell the group that their job is to check their knowledge of people skills by seeing how many other words describing an interpersonal skill they can make from the letters in the term *people skills*. Each of the words must use only the letters in *people skills* and must contain either a *p* or an *s*.

Allow five minutes for this part of the activity and then ask each team to pick out one of their words. They will then prepare a three-minute lesson on that particular item.

Discussion Questions

1. How many words did most of you find?

2. How many of you identified some words that may not often be associated with people skills?

3. What were some of the more unusual words found?

4. Can you think of some acronyms that might have been used?

What's in a Name? (Part 2)

Directions

In the area of people skills, we all know a number of individual traits or characteristics that exemplify what these interpersonal skills are all about. Your team's task is to find as many words as you can using only the letters in the term *people skills*. Each word you find must include either a *p* or an *s*. Then, be prepared to present a three-minute lesson on one of these words to the other teams.

PEOPLE SKILLS

_____   _____   _____

_____   _____   _____

_____   _____   _____

_____   _____   _____

_____   _____   _____

_____   _____   _____

_____   _____   _____

_____   _____   _____

_____   _____   _____

NOTES

_____

_____

_____

_____

_____

_____

_____

_____

_____

_____

_____

_____

Take a Card, Any Card (Part 2)

OBJECTIVE
- To be used as a get-acquainted activity

Materials

Participants' business cards

Time

5 to 10 minutes

Procedure

Ask participants to find another person in the group that they do not know (or perhaps don't know very well). Have them exchange business cards and tell the other person something about themselves and their job. Then, ask them to tell how their present position is different from what they were doing a year or two ago.

Have them describe to their partner how they are doing more now than before and what new skills they have developed over the past few months. How did they get help? From whom? How will their job be changing over the next several months?

Switch partners as time allows.

Discussion Questions

1. Did any of you find some job responsibilities in common?

2. How many of you have duties now that were not even thought about a year or two ago?

3. How did you find the help you needed to take on your added responsibilities? How can we help you right now?

4. What do you see down the road for your job? What are you going to do to prepare for it?

4

Communication Skills

I know you think you understand what I meant, but I'm not sure what you heard is what I intended to convey—I think.

—*Anonymous*

"But that's not what I meant . . . !"

"How come nobody ever listens around here?"

"But that's not what you said, was it?"

Sound familiar? If so, you're in good (or perhaps not-so-good!) company. Doesn't it seem a bit strange that with today's technology we can literally communicate around the world in a matter of few seconds, yet it may take minutes, weeks, months, or even longer to really "get through" to the person in the next cube or office?

This chapter will explore some of the reasons why this may be the case. We'll look at how much time we tend to spend in communication and how good we are at it. You'll also learn some tips on how to improve your listening skills, and in general be able to improve your own expertise as well as those of your attendees and audiences.

Definitions

Ask your participants to define *communication* and you'll likely get as many answers as there are people in your group.

Webster's definition is "to convey; to impart; to converse" and further, "to cause to be common to others; to share with others."

We could go on, but you get the point. How's this sound for starters? "Communication is the mutual exchange of information and understanding by any effective means." Note that this definition mandates both information and understanding—easier said than done. It also states that the vehicle for communication can take many forms, i.e., "by any effective means." This could be e-mail, Skype, iPhones, or virtually any new technology coming on board down the line. It also infers that the method may be totally nonverbal. The saying "Your actions speak so loudly, I can't hear a word you're saying" is apropos and to the point. Doubtless, we've all seen cases where body language speaks volumes. For example, a raised eyebrow or quizzical look on one of your participants may suggest you need to go back and restate your premise. Allow time for questions to make sure you are indeed communicating effectively.

Importance

Have you ever thought about how much time we all "communicate" in any given day? Studies at major universities have investigated this for some time and have shown that the average person (whomever that might be!) spends at least 70 percent of their waking hours in some form or phase of communication. In other words, you and your attendees are spending well over half your day reading, writing, listening, or speaking.

Interestingly enough, the higher a person rises in his or her organization, the more time that person spends in communication. Keep in mind that the 70 percent mentioned above is for the *average* person. In all likelihood, the figure will be closer to 80 or 90 percent. You could easily make the argument that if we throw in "nonverbal" to the mix, that figure hits the 100 percent mark.

Couple that with other research in this field that suggests that while most of us spend about 70 percent of our time in communication, we do so at about a 30 percent efficiency rate! In other words, for many of us, 70 percent of our training or speaking efforts can be misunderstood, misinterpreted, mistaken, missed, or messed. Seventy percent can be distorted, disdained, disputed, or dissented by our participants. However, make no mistake—if handled correctly, this dissonance can be turned in your favor.

In other words, you cannot *not* communicate. Forgive the double negative, but the point is a valid one. We all tend to "read" others and, though they may not say word one, they are still communicating by virtue of their body language and kinesics.

Goals

It would be presumptive to think that every time we communicate we need to have some kind of objective or goal in mind. Clearly, we simply don't have time to do so. However, it still is important to review some of the general goals of communication and see if they don't resonate with you and your attendees.

1. **To get action.** Certainly, you want some result or ROI on the time and effort you spend communicating. Most of us don't do this of course, and we're not advocating that every phone call, e-mail, or BlackBerry message need to have a specific goal in mind. Management has been defined as the "art of getting things done through others." Let's massage that just a bit by suggesting it is the art of "getting the right things done through others." Why is it that in today's fast-paced and hurried workweek, many of us never have time to do the things we need to do—but always make time to go back and do them over again? That "haste makes waste" is an all-too-true adage.

2. **To give/get information.** Note the two-pronged sword. Sure, we want to impart information and content to our attendees and audiences, and that is clearly part of what our jobs are all about. But simply tossing out facts and figures, i.e., "information," is not really communicating. Going back to our definition, unless there is understanding by way of feedback, performance, and so on, how can we be sure there is any type of response or learning on their part? Without question this type of one-way communication is not communication at all.

   On the other hand, the "getting" part is equally important. This feedback takes many forms with your attendees. The question-and-answer portions, as well as other types of audience participation and involvement, can help ensure the communication is indeed two-way.

3. **To motivate; to persuade.** As trainers, meeting professionals, and speakers, part of our task is "selling" ideas to the group. As learners, we all learn from one another. While we all know that motivation is an internal function, we can set the stage for learning by reviewing some of the basics of adult learning concepts.

   With today's Gen Xers and Gen Yers, telling is not the same as effective training. They have a strong need to take part in their own learning and, as such, have a right—and even a responsibility—to question their presenters. Be prepared for their questions and make them an integral part of your program. (Incidentally, even though they may not be challenging you verbally, they may be doing so even more emphatically with their text messages and tweets to their fellow participants.)

4. **To give/get understanding.** Remember, there is simply no real communication unless there is understanding and an acknowledgment of understanding on the part of the listeners and attendees. Whether this is done through some kind of formalized testing, pop quizzes, or feedback forums, it is important to allow plenty of time in your sessions to make sure they are all on the same page.

Barriers

If indeed our communication sometimes misses its mark, what are some of the obstacles or barriers that stand in the way? As we mentioned earlier we are all too familiar with Murphy's Law—"Whatever can go wrong will." Many of us also know the corollary—O'Toole's Law, which states that "Murphy was an optimist."

Let's review a few of the more common roadblocks that stand in our path to more effective communication:

1. **People.** Yup, as Pogo so eloquently stated, "We have met the enemy and he is us." Has there not been a time or two when we have been our own worst enemy? Maybe we just didn't spend enough time in preparation for that new program, or forgot that our group already knew a good bit of the content we were presenting. Maybe we're talking to them in a condescending manner or perhaps not really addressing the learning styles of our diverse audiences.

   "Tell Carol to tell Mike to make sure Beth gets this message." Sure they will—or not! Anytime we involve another person or two in the communication process, it tends to increase the possibility of misunderstanding. You've all seen it happen—each of us tends to listen or hear things from our own perspective and puts it through a type of filtration system. What the second person hears may bear little resemblance to the original message. By the time it gets down the chain, most of the intent may have been distorted or completely lost in the process.

2. **Assumptions.** "But I thought you meant..." As already mentioned, our assumptions often get in the way of true meaning. We all listen from our own points of view and often make snap judgments. Remember the well-worn phrase, "Don't confuse me with the facts; my mind is already made up."

3. **Semantics.** This includes jargon, acronyms, and a host of other items. The average word in the English language has around 25 different meanings. As an example, the word *round* has more than 70 different meanings. As a simpler example, suppose your manager asks for this report on a "bimonthly" basis. What does she mean? Check it out—it could mean twice a month or every two months.

Listening

In the previously mentioned studies regarding the effectiveness of the communication process, we identified a 30 percent success ratio. While a 30 percent figure is considered very good for a baseball player (that's a 300 batting average), it is simply not good enough for any of us working with people. And those "people" we're referring to include everyone with whom we come in contact. In other words, that means our attendees, our colleagues, our friends and family, and everyone else on the planet with whom we have some connection.

Let's face it. Many of us don't really listen as well as we could or should. While we can always give excuses—"I was really busy at the time," "She really didn't catch my attention," or dozens of other feeble reasons—it is incumbent upon us as trainers, facilitators, speakers, and meeting planners to help ourselves and our participants to improve that "batting average."

Someone once mused that "we have two ears and one mouth, which could be a subtle hint that we should listen twice as much as we talk." Easier said than done. Clearly, part of our jobs as speakers and trainers is to impart new information. Hence, we could argue that we should be talking more. However, that is a really weak premise. Our learners and attendees want to have an active part in their learning, and active and substantive discussion is a key to better learning. As point of fact, one of the laws of adult learning, called the Law of Exercise, states that the more we get our participants involved and engaged, the better the learning—both long and short term.

So, if we do agree that we could all improve our listening skills, how do we go about it? For starters, try these on for size:

1. **Stop talking.** Wow, what a concept! Give others equal time to have their say. While some may be able to speak and listen at the same time, for most of us it just doesn't work that way.
2. **Listen between the lines.** Surely we want to make sure we "hear" what the other person is saying, but consider what is perhaps being inferred by that person's statements. We all know the importance of nonverbals, and oftentimes actions do speak louder than words.
3. **Tune in.** Make certain you are giving more than lip service to other people. Actively listen and make sure you're on the same wavelength with them. Pay close attention and be certain that your own nonverbals show that you are really interested in their comments.
4. **Give immediate feedback.** Probably nothing is more important than this suggestion. Before you respond to others, take a moment and tell them what you thought they said. This may sound like trivial advice, but it can save time and headaches later on. Try saying, "Now, what I heard you saying is . . ." or, "In other words, what you want is . . ." There are dozens of variations. Find one that fits your comfort zone.

Summary

This chapter reviews some of the basics of effective communication. For many of us, the majority of our time is spent in some form or phase of communication. Whether it is a one-on-one conversation, a training program or presentation we're delivering, or "conversing" by text, Twitter, or Blackberry to someone halfway around the world, it is imperative we review these ideas and make sure our attendees do the same.

Like anything else, the best way to improve is to review these suggestions and put them to use in your everyday activities. Then "just do it!"

E-Mails for Business

Materials

PowerPoint slides or flip chart, copies of the E-mails for Business handout (provided), pens or pencils

Time

15 to 20 minutes

Procedure

Use a PowerPoint presentation or flip chart to demonstrate sample e-mails. (Use the material provided in the E-mails for Business handout for the samples.) Distribute copies of the handout for each person to work on independently. After each person completes the handout (approximately five to six minutes), the trainer will review each question with the group and provide the correct answers and explanation.

Discussion Questions

1. What is the first change you will now make with your e-mails?

2. What errors have you been making and how can you change them?

3. Do you think there should be a format for business e-mails similar to the way we were taught about a professional business letter format?

E-Mails for Business

Directions

E-mails are now the main format for business communication. How you present and send e-mails is a reflection on you and your company. Answer the questions below as they relate to your business correspondence. Circle the letter next to the best answer.

1. If you are sending an e-mail to a business contact and you are responding back and forth, on the fourth or fifth e-mail in the chain, is it still necessary to address your recipient with *Hello* or *Dear*?

    a. Yes

    b. No

2. What should your signature line consist of?

    a. Full name

    b. Address

    c. Phone

    d. E-mail

    e. Web site

    f. All of the above

3. How should a thank-you be handled? Will a text message or e-mail suffice?

    a. Send the initial quick thank-you through e-mail, but then follow up with a handwritten note.

    b. Only send an e-mail.

    c. A quick text message is just fine to say thanks.

4. If you receive an e-mail from an associate announcing a new promotion or job change, how do you handle sending a note of congratulations?

    a. Just respond to all on that e-mail and express your sincere congratulations so all can see how excited you are for this person.

    b. Send the person a handwritten note.

    c. Only respond to the sender on that e-mail and wish that person well.

    d. Both b and c

5. If you are returning from a meeting or out of the office, and you start to read your e-mails, should you automatically just start to reply to these e-mails?

    a. Yes, respond as quickly as possible starting at the most recent e-mail.

    b. You are busy, so just get to the e-mails at your earliest convenience.

    c. Review all the e-mails you received while you were gone before responding.

6. You receive a joke or a chain letter that you want to share. You never usually send these through your business e-mail address, so you feel this one time won't hurt.

    a. Not a problem; a few chain letter e-mails and/or jokes are acceptable.

    b. You should think twice regarding your company's policies regarding e-mail before ever using this mode of communication for personal material.

    c. You can't remember any policies in the company handbook relating to e-mail, phone, or other forms of personal communication, so this is fine.

7. You need to discuss poor conduct or even a termination with an employee, so you send him or her an e-mail.

    a. Not a problem at all because you know it needs to be placed in written form in the employee's personnel file, and this way you can just avoid that extra step.

    b. The employee will appreciate this procedure to avoid confrontation.

   c. E-mails should not be used as a substitute for discussing important matters that should take place in person or at least over a phone.

8. You receive an e-mail that there has been a change in a meeting time that asks all participants to check for other times they may be available. The sender asks you to respond so he or she knows that you received this notification and will handle it accordingly. Do you just respond to the sender or include all the recipients to advise of your schedule?

   a. Respond only to the sender.

   b. Respond to all so they are also aware of your schedule and possible availability.

9. You have been going back and forth several times with an associate via e-mail and finally decide on a time and location for your meeting. What would be your response back to this person to confirm the final details?

   a. That would be great, see you then.

   b. OK.

   c. Sounds great, and I'll meet you on Tuesday, October 6th at 11:30 A.M. at Rick's Restaurant on Main Street.

10. The subject line could be the most important part of your e-mail. It will be read before the body of the e-mail, and possibly encourage the reader to open it first over the tons of other e-mails he or she receives. What are some key factors of the subject line?

   a. Grab their attention. Have a hook.

   b. Alter and update your subject line as you progress throughout the business transaction.

   c. Never just state "hi" or leave the subject line blank.

   d. All of the above

E-Mails for Business Answers

1. A. Yes, this is a business communication and your e-mails, or portions of them, may be sent on to other people and they must always look professional and not casual.

2. F. Make it easy for people to always contact you. Avoid excessive designs and colored backgrounds. Just the facts!

3. A. If a gift of flowers or a basket of goodies is sent, the sender always wants to know if it was received. A quick phone or e-mail thank-you works, but then follow up with a handwritten note.

4. D. C is sufficient, but a handwritten or congratulatory note is always appreciated.

5. C. Review all e-mails before responding. The sender might have sent several and could have already provided the information you are seeking.

6. B. You are on company time and they are not paying you for personal e-mails.

7. C. All important matters should be handled face-to-face or on a private phone call.

8. A. Only the sender needs to know this information for planning purposes.

9. C. You have discussed various times, locations, and dates, so include the final details in your confirmation e-mail.

10. D. All of these are important when sending your e-mails. The subject line must grab, provide changes, and explain the body of the message.

Speed Dating: Do You Have a Minute?

OBJECTIVE
- To help attendees become comfortable with one another and to learn a little about their coworkers or associates

Materials

One long table where all participants can be seated on both sides; stopwatch; whistle, buzzer, or music player (e.g., CD player or iPod with speakers)

Time

10 to 60 minutes (depending on size of group)

Procedure

Similar to the speed dating from the movie *Hitch* with Will Smith, this is a great opportunity for members of an organization to get to know one another. It is also an excellent way for attendees to create or brush up on their "elevator speech" (a 30- to 60-second blurb about who they are and what they do). This activity is extremely effective if the group will be together for a full day to two. It allows them to find similarities within their group and to create a cohesive working relationship. It is amazing what 60 seconds can do when trying to make connections. Make it exciting and include all levels of management.

Have all attendees take a seat around the table. Explain that they will be given 60 seconds to meet the person across the table from them. They will shake hands, introduce themselves to one another with their short elevator speech, and provide one people skills tip to their partner.

Use the whistle, buzzer, or music to mark the beginning and end of the 60 seconds. At the end of the 60 seconds, everyone will get up and move to their right. Once the signal is sounded again, the next round begins. Make the whistle, buzzer, or music enjoyable instead of an annoying shrieking sound. It is fun to use music representing each generation in your group. Just make sure the songs are fun, recognizable, and fit the demographics and will encourage them to get up and move around the table.

If the group is extremely large, then several areas or tables can be used.

Discussion Questions

1. Were you able to perfect your elevator speech?
2. Are you able to remember at least one thing about each person or would you at least be able to recognize each person if you met him or her again?
3. How much can you discover about a person in 60 seconds?
4. How did each person differ in presenting him- or herself?

"Hi, My Name Is . . ."

OBJECTIVE
- To show that "actions speak louder than words" and that nonverbals can communicate effectively

Materials

None needed

Time

10 to 12 minutes

Procedure

Nonverbal communication is an integral part of the communication process. To prove this, you will ask your group to see how well they can introduce themselves to a new friend strictly by using nonverbals. Ask participants to find another person in the group that they have not met before today. If the group members all know one another, ask them to select someone they don't know all that well. Their job is to introduce themselves to their colleague and tell that person as much as they possibly can in two minutes' time. They can be as creative as they like, by showing pictures and so forth—but the only caveat is that everything must be done nonverbally.

After two minutes, have the partners switch roles and repeat the process. Do not yet process. After the additional two minutes, ask the group to discuss what they thought their partners were telling them.

Discussion Questions

1. When you "read" your partner's nonverbals, was it fairly easy to figure out what that person was "telling" you?

2. As you interpreted your partner's nonverbals, were there some gestures that made absolutely no sense to you?

3. As you think about your job, what are some suggestions you can offer that would help improve one's nonverbals?

Once Upon a Time . . .

Materials

None needed

Time

10 to 15 minutes

Procedure

Suggest that often we can communicate with others by nothing more than some nonverbal gestures and actions. Ask the group to form into teams of two or three. Tell them to think of a story or experience from their early childhood days. These might take the form of their first day in school, a favorite fairy tale, a family vacation, a visit to a relative's home, or some other early memory. Their task is to figure out how they can relate that particular story to their partner(s) by using only nonverbal signals and gestures.

Allow each person on the team three or four minutes to relay his or her individual story—in total silence, where not a single word is spoken aloud. Following this, have each team debrief, checking how others read their body language.

Discussion Questions

1. When you told your story, was it easy to construct and organize your thoughts? Was it fairly easy to get it organized?

2. When you were thinking of your stories, did it bring back some memories that you had not even thought about in years?

3. As you "read" your partner's nonverbals, did you find it easy or difficult to "get the picture"?

4. What are some suggestions you can offer that would help improve one's non-verbal communication efforts?

Text Messaging Shorthand

OBJECTIVE
- To teach you a new world of shorthand for a quick and easy way to send out nonbusiness communication messages

Materials

Copies of Text Messaging Shorthand handout (provided), pens and pencils

Time

10 to 15 minutes

Procedure

In our world of texting and electronic devices, we have created a quick and easy way to send our messages in the shortest amount of time. Is this correct for our business communication? Of course not. But it is a quick way to communicate with a friend. The list could go on and on with these abbreviated words. You never know when these few letters might help you. And, just so you know, PAL stands for "parents are listening."

You can either have the participants work on the handout individually or in groups. It might be helpful to have the different generations working together.

Discussion Questions

1. Did you even know that this shorthand existed?

2. Are you going to take the time to learn the abbreviated writing?

3. Do you see this as a positive or a negative?

Text Messaging Shorthand

1. *S	2. 10Q	3. 121	4. 143	5. 14AA41
6. 2BZ4UQT	7. 4COL	8. 511	9. 9	10. 99
11. @TEOTD	12. A3	13. AFK	14. BBL	15. CM
16. LOL	17. MOS	18. N/M	19. PCM	20. TYVM
21. TTYL	22. TTFN	23. TYLAS	24. UR2K	25. UG2BK

Answer Sheet

1. _____

2. _____

3. _____

4. _____

5. _____

6. _____

7. _____

8. _____

9. _____

10. _____

11. _____

12. _____

13. _____

14. _____

15. _____

16. _____

17. _____

18. _____

19. _____

20. _____

21. _____

22. _____

23. _____

24. _____

25. _____

Text Messaging Shorthand Answers

Answers going left to right starting on the top horizontal row.

1. Starbucks

2. Thank you

3. One to one

4. I love you

5. One for all and all for one

6. Too busy for you cutie

7. For crying out loud

8. Too much information

9. Parent is watching

10. Parent is no longer watching

11. At the end of the day

12. Anyplace, anywhere, anytime

13. Away from keyboard

14. Be back later

15. Call me

16. Lots of love / laughing out loud

17. Mom over shoulder

18. Nothing much

19. Please call me

20. Thank you very much

21. Talk to you later / type to you later

22. Ta-ta for now

23. Love you like a sister

24. You are too kind

25. You've got to be kidding

Source: NetLingo.com

5

Motivating Others

Always do what you are afraid to do.

—Ralph Waldo Emerson

When talking about motivation or motivating others, most people will say it is to energize or to be energized. When you listen to other trainers or speakers, you may instantly want to buy their ideas or products and start their new motivational program that will make you richer, smarter, and skinnier or to help you advance in your career or personal life. While all this might be true, there is a lot more to motivation than an instant fix.

We all vary tremendously regarding our motivational levels. Some motivation comes naturally and is inbred by our family members. Motivation can be caused by others constantly telling us to do well, work harder, eat less, exercise more, save money, be neat, be kind to others, honor your friends and family, and always do the best that you can. Some of these skills and motivators will come naturally, some we will drop off along the way, and others will only grow stronger.

Some people stay motivated by constantly trying to reach that pot of gold at the end of the rainbow, achieve a reward or monetary gain, or just reach a goal that they have set for themselves. This is all good, but what happens along the way as we reach for that golden ring in the circle of life?

Theories of Motivation

Motivation comes in many shapes and sizes including intrinsic and extrinsic motivation. The classic theories of Abraham Maslow, Frederick Herzberg, and Douglas McGregor are just a few examples. The basic theory of motivation is for people to do something so they can either achieve a reward or a positive end result. Motivation also makes people work for the opposite end, which is to avoid things they do not want.

But, with any of these theories, you must remember that what one person wants and values as a motivation to do well and achieve more could be at the very bottom of the totem pole for another person. People are not motivated by the same things. It all depends on where they are in their life, both personally and in their career, and where they want to go. Motivation varies and changes according to various wants, needs, goals, and happiness at that particular time in their life. Some things may never change, such as the motivation to eat, exist, achieve more in work, pay the rent or mortgage, and have a happy and healthy life and family. Other motivational factors will change as you change, grow older, and reach a time in your life when what motivated you years prior has a different meaning for you now.

Theories help us explain and determine what we may want and need, and classify these desires in order of their importance. Maslow created a hierarchy of needs, stating you start with the lesser needs before moving on to achieve the higher needs. He feels you need food and shelter and basic needs met before you can move on to more lofty goals. And once the need is met, it may no longer be a motivating factor.

Intrinsic motivators work for their own advancement and pure satisfaction. These are internal and value-based rewards. For people who are motivated intrinsically, money is not the end result but becomes an extrinsic motivator and they begin to lose interest and their motivation. There are people who only work and strive for extrinsic motivation—for the glory, the money, and the fame. Extrinsic motivators want tangible rewards. You can have both theories, but the intrinsic motivators rate higher on the Maslow hierarchy.

Herzberg's two-factor theory of motivation distinguishes between "motivators" and "hygiene factors." The motivators, such as challenging work, responsibility, and recognition, give positive satisfaction, while hygiene factors, including job status and security, salary, and benefits, do not motivate the person but, if not achieved or absent, would act as a demotivator. This theory has also been referenced as the motivation-hygiene theory and/or the dual-structure theory. Even though Herzberg did most of his original work in the late 1950s and '60s, it is amazing how well his theory holds up today. Tangible items have changed, of course, over the past 50 years, but job satisfiers as they relate to the factors involved in doing your job have pretty much stayed the same, and the job dissatisfiers are not necessarily the opposing reaction to the same factors.

McGregor's theory X and theory Y describe two different managerial approaches to worker motivation. In theory X, managers believe that workers inherently dislike work and are only in it for the money. In theory Y, managers use praise and recognition as much stronger motivators than money. McGregor states that motivated employees will always look for a better way to do their job, are more quality oriented, and are more productive employees.

All of these theories have their challenges, but no matter the theory, the purpose, or the end result, people are motivated for various reasons and by differing goals and will achieve a variety of successes in their life for both personal and professional goals and achievements.

How the leader, supervisor, manager, or owner of a company plays a role in all these factors can and will be critical. They determine how their team will work with them and their company as well as the end result. Their praise, trust, leadership, treating workers as equals, motivation, and belief in their employees will create the team that they want and need. This in turn will create a domino effect throughout the company and will continue their work starting at the top and continuing throughout the entire organization. Every year a list of the top 100 places to work throughout the United States appears in *Fortune* magazine. Thousands of employees state why they enjoy working for a particular company. Among the top five responses has been that their company creates a place where people *want* to work as opposed to *having* to work. If companies create a place where people want to work, they will achieve better profits, better customer relations and satisfaction, and better financial results.

How do these companies create a great work environment? They communicate by asking their employees what they want; they lead but don't dictate; their values are high; they achieve what they set out to do; and they motivate their employees. In times of economic downturn, we may experience the most crucial need for great leadership and motivation. This is also when companies especially need loyal, dedicated employees who believe in the company's goals and will accomplish whatever is necessary to make them happen, which makes the company stronger and more productive. As one of the top 100 companies stated, "We choose to operate on faith, not fear."

Motivate to Get Results

People use different tactics to make certain things happen. Some people are fortunate with the talent and ability to not only keep themselves motivated but to motivate people around them. They do this through special skills, communication, and incentives, including the following:

- **Enjoyable job and workplace.** As stated above, make it a place where people want to work.
- **Incentives.** Incentives do not need to cost hundreds or thousands of dollars. You would be surprised what makes people happy. Generally there are few costs involved.
- **Clear guidelines and instructions.** Give instructions and let them take over.
- **Goals.** Set them, check on them, and make them happen.
- **Courtesy through kindness and respect.** That is the basis for tremendous success. It is amazing how simple kindness is often overlooked.
- **Time lines with deadlines and checkpoints.** Some people work best with direction. No matter the generation, there are those who still want and need direction. They need to be informed with structured goals, time lines, and deadlines.
- **Team spirit and responsibilities.** We don't all need to be in a circle, holding hands and singing "Kumbaya," but it could be a fun exercise!
- **Kudos and achievement recognition.** Time after time, praise and recognition rank higher than monetary rewards. Think about it: just giving an employee a note of thanks for a job well done, or announcing at a staff meeting what a great job a certain individual or department did, could boost morale and motivate employees more than the ham or turkey offered to them over the holidays, or the slight raise they may receive at the end of the fiscal year.

- **Personal involvement.** We all need to feel ownership, partnership, and a buy-in to the company we work. Again, it doesn't need to be financial buy-in, but a pride in ownership that our job plays a role in the end result.
- **Empowerment.** If you don't trust them to do a job, why did you hire them? Give them the responsibility to complete a job or project and then walk away. Allow them to come to you with questions or set various checkpoints, but set the parameters and let them go.
- **Trust.** Again, if you don't trust them, they shouldn't be a part of your organization. Let them grow and empower them to make certain decisions that fit their job area.
- **Challenges.** Set the bar high enough that they are always trying to make it up one more step on that challenge ladder, or just high enough that their job does not become a routine. This way they are motivated to work harder and to prove themselves for a possible advancement or recognition.
- **Creativity.** People will amaze you if you allow them to express their creativity. Some ideas may not be worth changing a program to accommodate or spending thousands of dollars on, but who knows? They may have exactly what you are looking for or need. But, if you don't allow free thinking, you will never know.
- **Constructive criticism.** Do people like to hear criticism? Of course not. But if it is delivered quickly and effectively, then it is helpful and will provide the means for employees to grow, become more effective, and act efficiently.
- **Achieve improvement.** If you don't tell them, chances are they will not know. A lot of people do not set their goals high enough. They can get to a point where they think you are happy, so they stay on this road. But, as a leader, from time to time you need to raise that bar just a little higher. Keep their goals within reach but with a lot of work.
- **Fun and positive feedback.** This is the ultimate goal. Everyone wants fun and positive satisfaction for a job or project well done. Keep it coming and the harder and better they will work. People deep down want to feel good and make other people happy for what they have

done. By providing positive kudos, you will make their job more fun, and you will receive the positive end results over and over again.

- **Advancement opportunities.** Although not all do, most people want to advance. Some are content in their little comfort zone, but is that the best place for them? Do they have the abilities and talent to serve your company better in a different position or role? While only some employees are constantly looking for the next advancement, you need to keep a balance and excitement for all employees.
- **Exciting jobs, no matter how long the employment.** This can be a challenge. So what does make the job and the role of that employee exciting? This is the role you need to be involved in as either the employer or the employee. What do you want in this job, and what can you give that employee in this job? Think communication, involvement, happiness, and motivation.

Job Motivation Factors

What motivates people to work? What skills do they need to succeed? What is important to motivate them to do the very best that they can?

- A safe and secure job—this can be difficult with the uncertainties of the economic pressures, but being in a positive and encouraging environment will help them do their job to the best of their abilities.
- Respect for them in the workplace
- Good pay for the job they are doing
- Ability to be promoted
- A voice in staff meetings and office discussion
- Trust and respect from supervisors
- Empowerment to handle a job without constant supervision
- Good working conditions including effective technology and resources
- Feeling like a team player
- Ability to be creative
- Communication throughout the company
- Receiving kudos from supervisors for a job/project well done

The Pygmalion Effect

The basis of the Pygmalion effect is that if you believe someone can achieve anything they want, then they will. This can happen anywhere—at school, at home, and especially in the workplace. This is also known as the "self-fulfilling prophecy." If you believe your team or an individual will perform well and accomplish whatever they want, then they will. If you don't believe in them, then they won't.

In Ovid's narrative poem *Metamorphosis*, Pygmalion, a sculptor in Cyprus, creates an ivory statue of his ideal and perfect woman. He calls her Galatea, and she is so beautiful that he falls in love with her. He begs the goddess Aphrodite to breathe life into the statue so he can have her as his wife. The statue does come to life, and Pygmalion and Galatea are married and live happily ever after.

Another version of this story that you may know is George Bernard Shaw's play *Pygmalion*. This play was turned into the musical *My Fair Lady*. Professor Henry Higgins makes a bet with his friend Pickering that he can teach a Cockney flower girl, Eliza Doolittle, to act like a duchess. Eliza tells Pickering that it doesn't matter what she is taught by the professor, but rather how she is treated by him.

We can all be taught how to dress properly or speak correctly; the difference is how we are treated. To Professor Higgins, Eliza Doolittle was always going to be a flower girl because that was how he viewed her. But, we know the end of the story and the Cockney flower girl did become a duchess.

In our workplace, a lot depends on you. You determine the performance of your employees and their level of excellence. If you expect the best, then that is what you will get. There is a great quote attributed to Johann Wolfgang von Goethe: "Treat a man as he is and he will remain as he is. Treat a man as he can and should be and he will become as he can and should be." If Goethe stated that two centuries ago, surely we can catch on by now and make it happen.

If you are the manager or supervisor of a department or the head of a team, you need to have expectations for the people that report to you. You need to communicate these expectations to these employees. Each person may read your expectations differently, but it all depends on how you treat them and what they feel is expected of them. These employees will perform and react to your expectations and the way you make them feel. Remember Eliza and how she was treated.

There is a great song by R. Kelly, "I Believe I Can Fly." The song states, "If I just believe it, there's nothing to it. I believe I can fly. I believe I can touch the sky. Hey, cause I believe in me." People do need to believe in themselves, and you can help them excel and succeed. Sending positive thoughts and expectations will only encourage their self-esteem. Once people believe they can fly, they will succeed and their performance level will reach not only their expectations, but yours and that of the company.

Summary

This chapter has reviewed some of the classic as well as contemporary research into the fascinating topic of motivation. While we have yet to fully understand that elusive "black box" that turns people on, we do know that "different strokes for different folks" is a skillful tool.

Little Black Box (Part 1)

Materials

Flip chart, PowerPoint slide, or handouts; paper; pens or pencils

Time

10 to 15 minutes

Procedure

Review the items under the "Motivate to Get Results" section earlier in this chapter. Prepare a listing of these on a flip chart, PowerPoint slide, or handout.

Divide the group into teams of four or five and ask them to review this list and add other items that they feel should be included. Then ask each team to list their top three motivating factors and to prepare a three- to five-minute presentation as to why they ranked them as they did.

Discussion Questions

1. Did your team seem to all buy into the top three items?

2. Did you find significant differences among the various age groups? If so, why?

3. How many of you identified some important items not even included in the items shown?

4. What are some ways you can use these findings at work?

5. What is the most important thing you learned from your colleagues?

Motivate One Another

OBJECTIVE
- To get participants to know a little more about the people in their office or group, while at the same time motivating themselves and the other participants

Materials

    3 x 5 note cards, pens or pencils

Time

    15 to 20 minutes

Procedure

As people enter the room, have them write their name on a 3 × 5 card and then present them with four additional blank cards. Break the group into teams of four or five. Participants will secretly write four things (one per card) that describe themselves or their characteristics. So that the players do not recognize each other's handwriting, have them write with the opposite hand they usually use or or some other trick. Each team's cards will then be collected and given to another team. Each team's job is to match the cards to the people on the other team.

Set a short period of time (five to six minutes) for everyone to guess the people and match their four characteristics. Then have one team at a time tell why they feel that person fits those characteristics.

Discussion Questions

1. Were you surprised how well you did matching the correct people to their own descriptions? Or the opposite, if you got most of them wrong?

2. Did any of the descriptions surprise you in regard to what people thought about themselves?

3. Were your cards correctly identified as belonging to you? If not, were you happy or disappointed by the words they thought described you?

Brain Teaser #2

Work with your team to decipher the hidden meaning of each box. See page ix for additional instructions.

1. HEA R T	2. HEAVEN –1cent –1cent –1cent	3. ohd8io	4. ACC4ENT
5. MANY COUNT MANY COUNT	6. take back _____ Investment	7. R I G H T	8. BLOWN$.25
9. funny funny words words words words	10. MEAL TALK	11. MOTDLEIFION	12. E/N/D
13. <u>FLIGHTS</u> booked	14. 1.ha 2.rm 3.on 4.y	15. TSTIIMTCHE	16. <u>HIGH</u> SWINE

Brain Teaser #2 Answers

1. Broken heart

2. Pennies from heaven

3. Dayton, Ohio

4. Foreign accent

5. Too many to count

6. Return on investment

7. Right up the middle

8. Blown to bits

9. Too funny for words

10. After-dinner speech

11. Backfield in motion

12. Split end

13. Flights overbooked

14. Four-part harmony

15. Stitch in time

16. High on the hog

6

Changing Generations

The greatest discovery of any generation is that a human being can alter his life by altering his attitude.

—William James

The increasing numbers of Gen Xers and Gen Yers in your meetings come with totally different expectations and learning styles. Since they have grown up with the newest and latest in technology, it is no secret that your presentation and facilitation skills must be up-to-date, relevant, and engaging. As the saying goes, "The talking head is dead!"

Look around your own office and organization—the demographics are clear. In all likelihood, the same is true of your own audiences. They are younger, extremely techno-savvy, probably better educated, and far more sophisticated. Their attention span is a short one and they have little patience in giving their attention to someone who simply can't hold their attention.

The Generation Gap

It might be helpful to review some of the demographics of our changing workforce and society as a whole. Although the nomenclature used to describe the various age groupings may be somewhat confusing, e.g., Gen Y or millennial, there is some agreement as to the general age and values of each.

As we have been told, this is the first time in history that four generations are working with one another in the workplace. The traditionalists are coming back to work; the baby boomers are working way beyond 60, 62, and 65 years of age; and Generations X and Y are playing major roles in the workforce.

The Traditionalists
These "seniors" or "veterans"—the group of "senior citizens" born before 1946—represent only a small portion of the workforce. Indeed, you are likely to find them doing volunteer service or greeting you at your neighborhood Walmart. They were brought up in an era where respect of others was the norm, and they tend to be very quite loyal to the "cause."

In general, the traditionalists are hardworking, are great team players, remain loyal to usually one company or field of work their entire life, respect and cherish their jobs, and work best with face-to-face communication and interaction.

The Baby Boomers
Born between 1946 and 1964, this group numbers around 70 million in the United States. They, too, are service oriented and even idealistic in their behavior. As good team members, they are often energetic and have high expectations.

Theirs is the generation of change and even rebellion. Baby boomers were post–World War II babies raised in the midst of Vietnam, bra burnings, streaking on college campuses, sit-ins, protests, and women's rights. Baby boomers feel obligated to work long hours, assume high levels of responsibility, are very committed and dedicated, and are motivated by incentives, praise, and challenges. They started the "workaholic" trend.

Generation X
When identifying the age groupings for Gen Xers, you may find some discrepancy as to just when this generation actually began. However, there is some consensus that Gen Xers were born between 1965 and 1979. Because many grew up in single-parent homes where a parent was away at work during the day, they are described as the "latchkey" generation. They tend to be comfortable working alone and not at all intimidated by authority figures. As point of fact, they may well tend to resist the formal atmosphere and structure of many organizations. They number around 45 million and they demand balance and fun in their everyday activities.

This generation is going back to family time and practices work/life balance. A lot of these mothers are now staying home with their children and/or working jobs that are part-time, have flexible hours, or can be handled from home.

Gen Xers are very creative and love diversity, challenges, and responsibility. If their job is not providing these opportunities, they will find an employer who can. Gen Xers prefer freedom, working alone, and reaching their goals in their own and efficient ways. This generation has an entrepreneurial spirit and is results oriented, self-reliant, and somewhat skeptical.

Face time and meetings are not important to them, and they prefer to work in ways that will challenge and motivate them.

Generation Y

Often referred to as "Generation Why?" this group was born between 1980 and 2000, and the "Gen Why?" label makes a correct statement. They tend to question authority—and sometimes everything else as well! However, contrary to popular opinion, this generation actually respects authority—but remember that this respect must be earned and shown. That same respect comes with performance not position. The term *millennial* is also used to describe this group. Also numbering around 70 million, they are very much at ease with all types of technology and welcome most any kind of change. They are self-confident and can seemingly take on many tasks simultaneously.

Gen Yers are the most tech-savvy since they have grown up with electronic gadgets since birth. They are the smart and creative generation and have received the most schooling, with some having as many as four or five years of preschool before ever making it to kindergarten. They look for challenges and ways to grow in their careers and find meaningful careers. They are the masters of multitasking and live and operate through technology. Face-to-face communication is not important to them and they operate more effectively and efficiently through e-mail, texting, and Web-based systems. Work/life balance is important to them, and providing other means to remotely connect through technology is the best for them. They will still provide the 24/7 required, but it needs to be through forms of technology.

The best way to work and motivate this generation is to provide structure, constant communication, and feedback. Praise is appreciated; they need to know the "why" of what is needed from them, and also assurance of how it could benefit them.

Managing a Multigenerational Workforce Is a Hot Topic

Nancy Barry, speaker, Gen Y expert, and author of *When Reality Hits: What Employers Want Recent College Graduates to Know,* feels that generational diversity is a good thing. Employers across the country are spending a tremendous amount of time trying to figure out how to get all the generations to work well together. She presents three ideas to create an environment of open communication, mutual respect, and collaboration.

- **Accept the fact we can all learn from other people's experiences and perspectives.** Everyone in the organization has something of value to bring to the table. There are times when it is hard to step aside and recognize that other people also have great ideas, but just because something has always been done a certain way doesn't mean it's the best way or the only way. We all need to be flexible and realize everyone has something to contribute to the success of the organization.
- **Focus on what you have in common.** We're spending too much time focused on the differences among the four generations. What if, instead, you focused on what you have in common? The one thing you all have in common is you are on the same team working toward one common goal—serving your customers and clients.

  Employees should treat every one of their coworkers with respect. It shouldn't matter how old they are, what position they hold, or how long they've been with the organization. All that really matters is the talent they bring to the organization. If managers want their people to treat colleagues with respect, employees need to see managers treating everyone in the organization with respect.
- **Get your colleagues talking to one another.** If you want a 59-year-old baby boomer to understand why a 24-year-old Gen Yer doesn't want to work all weekend, you need to get them talking to each other. If you want the 35-year-old Gen X employee to understand why he or she can't send a text message to a 70-year-old traditionalist, you need to get them talking.

  You may have days when you wonder if they are even talking the same language. If you ask someone on the team to send you a report by the end of the day, for a traditionalist or baby boomer that means 5 P.M. For a Gen Xer, it may mean 7 P.M. For your Gen Y employees, end of the day probably means 11:59 P.M. because that's what it meant during their college years.

Getting all the generations to work well together is not that hard. The key to success is to get all the employees to understand what's important to the other generations. Your people are your most valuable asset. Every success you have is because of your people. Period. If you get the people part right, everything else will fall in place.

For just a moment, pay no attention to titles, tenure, or job responsibilities. Forget how old your colleagues are. Think of people as just people. Take the time to understand them. Who are they? What do they value? What motivates them? What is their preferred communication style? Do they prefer face-to-face or electronic communication? If a colleague asks you to send them an update on a project, do they want a bullet-point update or a detailed overview? If your coworker is out of the office and you need to get a message to him or her, do you send an e-mail, leave a voice mail message, or send a text message? Your ability to answer these questions is key to your success.

The main reason there is tension between the generations is because most people don't know their colleagues on a personal level. What can you do to change that? Reach out to a member of another generation and get to know him or her. Find out what makes that person tick. Ask what drives him or her crazy about another generation and why. Make a commitment to respect each other, even if you don't see eye-to-eye on everything. After the meeting, follow up with a note to let your colleague know how much you enjoyed getting to know him or her. Will you send a handwritten note, e-mail, or text message? It will all depend on his or her preferred communication style.

Generational Diversity Is a Good Thing

The reality is you wouldn't want to work with a team where everyone looked like you, thought like you, and was the same age. Being different isn't right or wrong, it's just different. Your success is based on creating an environment of open communication, collaboration, and respect. Focus on the fact that everyone has something of value to offer. If you focus on talent, rather than age, wonderful things will happen.

Summary

So, armed with this data, how can we best make use of this information in our presentations and training programs? With this diversity not only in age and values, how can we be sure that we're meeting the expectations and needs of our attendees? Regardless of the age and interests of your audiences, you can rest assured that there indeed is one common thread among them. Namely, they want information—they want content and information that is relevant, timely, and practical. Don't bother wasting their time (and yours too) with trivial and outdated material. Get them involved with questions and allow plenty of time for their small-group discussions.

Build in time for them to get to know their fellow attendees. The importance of climate-setting and get-acquainted activities cannot be overstated. This collegiality is a great way to ensure that their social media needs can be addressed. At risk of redundancy, be certain to build in numerous activities and exercises that involve and engage your attendees.

Dealing with Different Generations: Do You Remember?

Materials

PowerPoint slide or copies of Dealing with Different Generations: Do You Remember? handout (provided); judges; buzzers, horns, whistles, or some form of signal; pens or pencils

Time

10 to 15 minutes

Procedure

Members of each generation have a special person, song, movie, or event that they relate to. If asked, they can tell you exactly where they where or what they were doing when this particular event or incident happened. It is interesting to bring our generations together to get their perspective on specific times and places, no matter the decade or significance.

Divide participants into teams. Try to have at least one person representing the four generations that are now in our workforce (Gen X, Gen Y, baby boomer, and traditionalist) on each team. An announcer or emcee will read the questions and each team will have a buzzer, horn, whistle, or some form of signal to announce that they have the answer. The judges will determine any conflicts with the answers or decide any ties.

Discussion Questions

1. Were you surprised how the different generations knew some of the answers?

2. How did the four generations work as a team?

3. Did one generation dominate by knowing the answers over all the areas of time and generations?

Dealing with Different Generations: Do You Remember?

1. Where, how, and what year did John F. Kennedy die?

2. Who was Uncle Jesse?

3. Name the four Beatles.

4. Name two of the Top Ten Electrical Gadgets according to various lists compiled for 2000–2010.

5. Who was the first golfer to hold all four major golf titles simultaneously by winning the Masters, the U.S. Open, the British Open, and the PGA Championship?

6. What year was the tragic explosion of the Space Shuttle *Columbia* over Texas?

7. Who won his seventh straight Tour de France in 2005?

8. What year did Hurricane Katrina strike the Gulf Coast and inundate the city of New Orleans?

9. Who were the two famous baseball players in the '90s who were fighting for the title of "Most Home Runs Ever in One Season?"

10. When cellular phones first came on the market in the 1990s, what was the average cost?

11. What decade made the New Kids on the Block, *NSYNC, and Backstreet Boys popular?

12. What year and where did Princess Diana of England die?

13. When did John Glenn make his first and last flights in space?

14. In the 1967 movie, what actor played the "graduate" who was seduced by an older woman (played by Anne Bancroft)?

15. What was the name of the little girl who was stuck in a well in Midland, Texas, for nearly 59 hours in October 1987?

Dealing with Different Generations: Do You Remember? Answers

1. President John F. Kennedy was assassinated in Dallas, Texas, on Friday, November 22, 1963.

2. There are actually two television characters with the name Uncle Jesse:

    a. Jesse Duke from *The Dukes of Hazzard* (1979–1985)

    b. Jesse Katsopolis from *Full House* (1987–1995)

3. John Lennon, Paul McCartney, George Harrison, and Ringo Starr

4. The Top Ten Electrical Gadgets according to various lists compiled for 2000–2010

    a. iPod (2001)

    b. BlackBerry (2002)

    c. Nintendo Wii (2006)

    d. PlayStation 3 (2005)

    e. iPhone (2007)

    f. Palm Pre (2009)

    g. Amazon Kindle (2007)

    h. USB Flash Drive (2000)

    i. Blu-Ray Disc (2006)

    j. Netbooks (2007)

5. Tiger Woods

6. February 1, 2003

7. Lance Armstrong on July 24, 2005

8. 2005

9. Mark McGwire (62 home runs beating Roger Maris's record of 61) and Sammy Sosa

10. $1,000

11. 1990s

12. August 31, 1997, in Paris, France

13. *Friendship 7* in 1962 and *Discovery* in 1998

14. Dustin Hoffman

15. "Baby Jessica" (Jessica McClure)

Little Black Box (Part 2)

Materials

None needed

Time

10 to 15 minutes

Procedure

Review the items listed earlier in this chapter outlining the four generations that are now working together in the workplace.

Divide the group into teams of four or five. On each team try to get as similar an age grouping—traditionalists, baby boomers, Gen Xers, or Gen Yers—as possible. If necessary, assign teams so that members of each team represent only one particular generation.

Ask each team to discuss what they believe to be important, i.e. the "black box," for a different generation. For example, a team of baby boomers may address what they believe is important for the Gen Yers; the Gen Yers may discuss what they think are important motivating factors for the Gen Xers; and so forth.

Then ask each team to report on what they believe would be the top three motivating factors for the generation they discussed. Following this, ask the actual members of that generation for their reactions.

Discussion Questions

1. Why did your team select the factors you did?

2. On what basis did you make these decisions?

3. Did you find differences of opinions among your team members? Why?

4. How can you use this information at work?

Brain Teaser #3

Directions

Work with your team to decipher the hidden meaning of each box. See page ix for additional instructions.

1. BILLED	2. DOUWINBLE ————— TIME	3. LAMOMW	4. COPS SCHOOL
5. 14$$$	6. GENƎRAL	7. TREHIDASURE	8. School retrauq
9. T M A U H S W T	10. talk	11. U P ————— 0	12. SLIGHTLY ————— CAST
13. OBSTACLES ————— COMING	14. ————— READING —————	15. LANG4UAGE	16. EGGS ————— EE E

Brain Teaser #3 Answers

1. Sick in bed

2. Win in double overtime

3. Mother-in-law

4. Police academy

5. One for the money

6. Attorney general

7. Hidden treasure

8. High school quarterback

9. What goes up must come down

10. Small talk

11. Split up over nothing

12. Slightly overcast

13. Overcoming obstacles

14. Reading between the lines

15. Foreign language

16. Eggs over easy

7

"Customer" Service

Do what you do so well that they will want to see it again and bring their friends.

—Walt Disney

As we mentioned in Chapter 3, the word "customer" is shown in quotation marks. Even if you're not directly serving "customers," likely you are serving someone else who is. We all have "customers" in one sense or another.

Customer Service: Disney Style

There are hundreds of theme parks and family entertainment centers around the world. These parks provide acres of thrilling rides, attractions, themed characters, animals, water, and much more. So, with all these choices, why is Disney always at the top of the list for a family to select for their vacation?

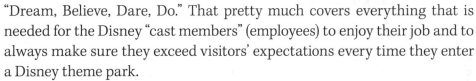

The key to Disney's philosophy is "Dream, Believe, Dare, Do." That pretty much covers everything that is needed for the Disney "cast members" (employees) to enjoy their job and to always make sure they exceed visitors' expectations every time they enter a Disney theme park.

The cast members strongly believe in attention to detail and they do "sweat the small stuff." With all the activities that are constantly happening in a large theme park, they base and assess all situations on safety, courtesy, customer service, and efficiency. You can take all of these elements and translate those to your job, no matter what you may be doing.

Think of all the times you have become frustrated with a company that wasn't providing service as promised or that sold you a poor-quality product. Probably you first get angry, then frustrated, and lastly even move on to another company or service. If you don't move on, then you are just another dissatisfied customer spreading the word about that company and your dissatisfaction. And with today's social media, half the world's population will hear about it!

Why do we allow this to happen? We should never be so set and locked into a pattern or a policy that we can't see what our customers want and need or what could make our coworkers more productive and creative and boost the morale of the entire company.

Treat Others How You Want to Be Treated

As trainers or meeting professionals, you enjoy working with people you like, and in turn, they like to work with you. Courtesy, kindness, and etiquette create the basis for customer service. Even if things go wrong with a project, a meeting, or an event, if you handle and solve the problem instantly, it is amazing how the majority of people will stay with you or your company because you still met—and even went beyond—their expectations. Loyalty is so necessary for strong customer satisfaction. You and your team are the only ones who can constantly wow your customers and build strong and lasting relationships.

Moments of Truth

As described in his book, *Moments of Truth*, Jan Carlzon became the leader of Scandinavian Airlines System (SAS) at a time when he hated life and was suicidal. The company was in huge financial trouble and the airline had a horrible reputation for lateness. You would think he would just throw up his hands and walk away, but instead he took the company and turned it around.

Carlzon was the first to use a separate cabin for business class but at the same time eliminated first class on all of SAS's European routes. Within one year SAS became number one in punctuality and started a training program called "Putting People First." It allowed the frontline employees to make decisions and resolve problems and issues right then and there. This changed the company's whole bottom line, tremendously increased its profits, and completely changed morale—so much so that SAS became Airline of the Year that following year.

Code of Quality Service

Management consultant and author Karl Albrecht stated that good customer service is an important part of any job. Whenever you come in contact with a customer, you create a "moment of truth." You determine your success in that moment, as it determines how that customer perceives you, the service you provide, and your overall company. These moments of truth set your service image.

Albrecht created 10 critical employee behaviors that will guarantee excellent customer service.

1. Greet the customer immediately.
2. Give the customer your complete attention.
3. Create a connection to the customer in the first 30 seconds.
4. Be natural, be yourself.
5. Be energetic and congenial.
6. Be a problem-solver for the customer.
7. Use common sense.
8. Be creative and original.
9. Use the last 30 seconds to add value for the customer.
10. Take good care of yourself.

All of these points can be used and reused. Try taking one of these tips and using it today with your customers. See how it makes a difference in your customer service style and the reaction you receive from your customers. Then after these 10 become second nature to you, start adding new ones that will fit you, your customers, and your company. It will be contagious because you will feel good about what you are doing, and your customers will have the faith and trust in you.

Customer Service–Driven Companies

Customer service is the key in many companies. One or two companies instantly come to mind when you think of which companies provide the ultimate in service to their customers. Just a few names that are synonymous with customer service are Southwest Airlines, Nordstrom, Houston Restaurant, Neiman Marcus, Marriott Hotels, and The Container Store.

Summary

The question is, what sets these companies apart from their competition and keeps their retention rate so high? But more importantly, how can you emulate these companies and their customer-service attributes? It all goes back to "treat others as you want to be treated"—a very simple statement. The service-driven companies feel good about themselves and they in turn make you feel good about yourself. It is a nice little cycle to be part of in both your personal and professional careers.

Moments of Truth

Materials
None needed

Time
10 to 15 minutes

Procedure

The "moment of truth" has been identified as the critical contact point between the customer and the sales/service person, between the planner and the supplier, and between the businessperson and the vendor when they make or break the sale.

Have your group break into teams of three or four. Ask each team to discuss among themselves recent "moment of truth" experiences. Have them provide positive examples, followed by any recent negative experiences.

Discussion Questions

1. Ask each group to share one or two examples of good customer service.

2. Without naming the firm or individual, provide an example of poor customer service. How could that situation be turned around to make it a positive situation?

3. What are some of the reasons that a company can be portrayed as having bad customer service?

Something You Like That Represents You

Materials

Whatever items the attendees wish to bring as "show and tell" OR drawing paper and markers or crayons

Time

15 to 20 minutes

Procedure

This activity is to represent the attendees with something they enjoy. It could be something they enjoy now, something they hope to enjoy and is on their "bucket list," or something they have enjoyed in the past. With the four generations in the workforce, it will be interesting to see if there is much variation.

If able to coordinate in advance, ask all attendees to bring or wear an item that they enjoy or that represents them. It could be a T-shirt from a concert or their alma mater, sports equipment, a costume, music, pictures—anything they enjoy. If unable to coordinate in advance, have drawing paper and markers or crayons available so they can instead draw the item or activity. This works equally well. Go around the room and have the attendees share a little about their item or drawing with the group.

Discussion Questions

1. Why is it so special and at the top of your list for enjoyment?

2. How does this item make you feel about yourself?

3. Has this always been something that makes you feel good, or has it changed over time?

Customer Service: No Is Not the Correct Word!

OBJECTIVE
- To instill with team members that no is not a good option when addressing a client or customer

Materials

3 x 5 cards, small box or bowl, 2 flip charts, markers

Time

15 to 30 minutes

Procedure

Have a sufficient list of challenges prepared on 3 × 5 cards placed in a small box or bowl. Depending on the size of the group, participants either will get a turn as a customer or employee presenting to the entire group or will work within smaller groups of 8 to 10 people and do their presentations only to that group.

Have participants pick a card that will list a challenge. The cards will state either "Employee" or "Customer" followed by a challenge. The first part of the activity is to find your partner with a matching challenge. The two matching people will act out the situation stated on the card for two to three minutes in front of the group.

No Unauthorized Dumping

Sample Card: Listing the Challenge

One person will act as the "Employee" and the other as the "Customer." Once the "Customer" states his or her situation, how does the "Employee" respond? How can they work this challenge out to the satisfaction to both?

"I've been placed on hold for the last 12 minutes trying to get an answer to my question regarding the upcoming meeting. Why can't someone help me?"

"I came into your offices last week to pick up my material and was told it was still on back order. I was promised delivery yesterday and my event is this weekend. I need some answers."

Using the above example, how, as the employee, can you handle this angry customer without jeopardizing future business, frustrating the customer even more, and providing positive answers even though you cannot deliver exactly what they want?

If this is a larger group and they have been working in smaller groups, save time at the end of the program for a few people to present their scenario to the entire group.

As a last part of this exercise, have a flip chart to write down negative words and phrases and a second flip chart to express the positive key words and phrases they should and could be using for the challenges and situations. The key words and phrases could then be given to everyone to have near their phone in their offices or near key areas as reminders.

Discussion Questions

1. If you were the customer, what are ways that you were turned around in a frustrating situation?
2. Name situations where you did turn a customer around and helped the customer understand the situation and how you were trying to handle it for him or her.
3. Are there situations where you have left a company due to the lack of customer service?

8

Business Etiquette

Good manners will open doors that the best education cannot.

—Clarence Thomas

It's hard to imagine, but etiquette has been in existence since prehistoric times when people started to interact with one another. Basically people skills and social conduct evolved over time to make life more pleasant and easier. What really brought etiquette to the forefront was a gardener in France back in the 1600s. During the reign of King Louis XIV, and the creation of the gardens of Versailles, the gardener was so particular and angry that people kept stepping on his gorgeous flowers that he placed signs, or *étiquets*, to keep them off the flowers. The meaning of *etiquette* would later include the ticket to court functions that listed the instructions on where a person would stand and what was to be done. This was truly the start, as we know it today, as a direction or a list of social behaviors.

Even though hundreds of years have passed, etiquette is still important. Yes, you should keep off the grass, but you should also know some basics including a good handshake, which bread and butter plate is yours, and proper business etiquette. These people skills of the twenty-first century are still signs of respect and kindness that will hopefully make your life easier and more pleasant.

Dining Skills

Eating is important, and most of us do it three or four times a day. Our society has changed over the centuries to a more fast-paced, multitasking society. Because of this lifestyle, our eating habits have suffered. The good news is that today's families are making an effort to have three to four meals each week together. It has been proven that children of families who eat meals together on a regular basis are healthier; less likely to smoke, drink, or use drugs; and have better scholastic scores and fewer behavioral problems. It's amazing what time together can do.

Dining Rules to Live By for Better People Skills

1. **Silverware.** The rule to remember is once you pick up any piece of your silverware, it never touches the table again. Don't let your silverware rest partially on the table and partially on your plate. Place the blade of the knife, the tines of the fork, or the bowl of the spoon facing the 10 o'clock position, as if visualizing your plate as the face of a clock. The bottom of the silverware will be at the 4 o'clock position. In most cases, work from the outside in with your silverware.

2. **BMW or the "b" and "d" rule.** To get your bearings when you are seated, think BMW—bread, meal, water. Your bread, meal, and water go left to right, just like the letters. Some people remember *b* for bread and *d* for drink. Make these letters by putting your index finger up in the air and then making a circle with your thumb and middle finger. Note that the lowercase letter *b* on your left hand facing the plate stands for bread and the lowercase *d* on your right hand facing the plate stands for drink. (The *d* sign is the actual *d* used in sign language.)

3. **The four- and five-letter trick.** The words *fork* and *left* both have four letters, so the forks go on the left side of your plate. *Knife* and *spoon* both have five letters and so does *right*, so they belong on the right.

4. **Hosts.** Take your cues from them. This includes where they may ask you to sit, when to place your napkin on your lap, when to start the meal, making toasts, discussing business, keeping pace with them while they are eating (to see if you need to slow down or speed up), when to finish the meal, when to place the napkin on the table, and when it's time to leave.

5. **When to start to eat.** Wait until everyone is served. If there are hosts, they either will start to eat or will make a gesture or comment for guests to enjoy the meal. When the host begins, you may also start. If a person at your table has requested a special meal, that

person should instruct everyone else at the table to begin since his or her meal may be delayed. Feel free to begin your meal.

6. **Double-dipping.** Never take a chip or hors d'oeuvre and dip it into a sauce or a dip, take a bite, and then dip it again. Either break the piece of food in half so you can dip both pieces or just dip the initial piece. Or if possible, place some of the dip on your own plate. You still shouldn't double-dip, but at least you are not all sharing the same food.

7. **Bread.** First place the butter on your plate. Do not go directly to the bread with the butter. Do not cut your bread but break it in half. Then break off only one bite-sized piece of bread at a time from the slice of bread or roll. Butter that piece, set the knife down on the plate, and then eat that one piece. Do not butter the whole roll or slice of bread (or even half) and then just start to bite off pieces.

8. **Salt and pepper.** Remember that salt and pepper are married. They go together. Even if someone asks you to pass just the salt, pick up both the salt and pepper and pass them together. Place them on the table next to the person and then he or she can select what is wanted. Do not hand them to the person making the request. When setting the table, put salt and pepper together at both ends of the table.

9. **Lipstick and makeup.** Don't apply makeup at the table or disappear under the table for a few seconds to put some on quickly. Just excuse yourself and go to the restroom to apply any lipstick, lip balm, lip gloss, or other touch-up if necessary during the meal.

10. **Toothpicks.** The rule on toothpicks is 1½. You'd better be 1½ miles from all people before that toothpick ever goes in your mouth. It's not cool to be walking out of a restaurant or a reception with a toothpick hanging out of your mouth.

Remember Julia Roberts in the scene from *Pretty Woman* with the food flying across the room? Well, that was cute for that scene, but you can't go to all those special social or business events with food orbiting around the room, or no idea if that is your fork or your neighbor's that you just picked up. After a while, the "cuteness" wears off.

The Age of Technology

Look around. Everyone has a cell phone, BlackBerry, or iPhone, no matter their age, the location, or the time of day. Walking down the street, in an airport, in the mall, in restaurants, waiting for a bus, or standing in line to get their morning coffee, everyone is on the phone. What are we doing? Can't we even go a few minutes without checking in with our office, our family, or our friends? Apparently not. So, if we must be totally connected at all times, at least be polite. Statistics show that cell phone users can be downright rude. The responses covered people talking too loudly, using phones in the wrong places, and continuing to talk on the phone while in the company of other people. There are proper people skills for utilizing any form of communication.

Here are our top 10 suggestions to hopefully provide a little civility for cell phone users:

1. **When you must take that call.** Think before you walk into a venue, restaurant, or someone's home. Make sure your phone is on vibrate if you have to keep it on. If you must take a call, excuse yourself and walk away to take the call. Be very quick and when you return, thank the person for allowing you to take that call.
2. **Don't scream.** You don't need to talk loudly when you are on your cell phone. Technology has advanced so that just normal talking will work. You may be enjoying your conversation on the phone, but other people around you do not need to hear all the details of your events of last night.
3. **Be aware of your surroundings.** People do enjoy a meal in a restaurant, going to a movie, attending church, or being at a sporting event without the person beside them constantly talking on the phone. Turn phones off completely. You can still enjoy that meal or event without using your cell phone, and just think how happy the people around you will be.
4. **The cell phone driver.** Several states have enacted the "nothing in the ear" law. This means no cell phone or ear adapter. It is terrifying to watch someone taking a turn wide, going over the median strip, or just plain swerving. Driving is a time to turn off that cell phone and

pay attention. Just because you insist of talking on your cell phone and driving doesn't give you the right to jeopardize the safety of other people on the road.

5. **Rudeness.** If you are with someone for a meal, in a car, or just in their company, then be in their company. Don't get on your phone. It's rude. When you are with another person, then be with that person.

6. **If you lose the call.** If you place a call and then are disconnected, or only catching every other word, then it is up to you to return the call. If you place the call, then you call back.

7. **The airplane.** Unfortunately, most airlines now allow people to turn their cell phones on when they hit the tarmac of the airport. Again, people instantly get on their phones to either tell the person picking them up the gate number or to continue a business meeting. This is great, but once again, people in Row 10 don't need to hear your conversation in Row 23. Talk softly. Everyone on the plane doesn't need to hear about your business deal or your fun vacation.

8. **The borrower.** Most phones offer free minutes, but don't ask to borrow a phone. It's tacky.

9. **BlackBerry.** It will vibrate and ring for e-mails, which can be annoying, so just turn this option off. It is just as impolite to be checking your e-mails during a meeting as it is to be taking calls.

10. **Warnings for cell phones.** Be aware of signage or announcements regarding cell phone use in hospitals, pharmacies, churches, restaurants, and so forth. Pay attention and do as asked.

The best suggestion is to turn off all electrical devices when in any of these environments. Remember the people around you.

A recent survey asked respondents if more time was spent on their home computer or with their spouse. Not surprisingly, 65 percent admitted they spent more time with their computer and only 35 percent with their spouse. It could be scary if they ask this question again a year or two from now.

Computerized office environments, telecommuting, and all the electronic innovations of the past two decades have created a new set of situations to challenge professional behavior and our people skills. As handy as some electronic tools can be, they also create irritation and interruptions. A business professional should know how to balance well-mannered attention to a client against a ringing cell phone. Shame on you if you don't!

E-Mail

E-mails might be the most used and the most common social faux pas. We send them quickly and in return expect a quick response. We now abbreviate and use shortened variations of words, and also feel that at any time or place it is appropriate to be checking e-mails, texting, and playing games. What happened to our etiquette, our kindness to the people around us, and the civility of being nice and respectful? We have allowed our multitasking environment to take us over.

Leading up to the 1990s, we always had a format for proper letter writing or the standard for our particular office or company. But, along came business-casual dress and the business-casual letter writer.

Guidelines to follow for a more professional e-mail:

- E-mail is still a business communication. Watch grammar, spelling, and abbreviations. People will judge your e-mail just as critically as they judge a business letter.
- Use the subject line. It may get your message read a little faster and the reader will be able to find the message for future referral. This could be the most important part of your e-mail and message.
- Don't use e-mail when a handwritten note is more appropriate.
- If you get a request addressed to numerous people, respond only to the sender unless requested to do otherwise.
- Read all your e-mails before responding. Go to the most recent ones first and you may discover earlier messages have been amended or updated.
- Be discreet about sending jokes and other questionable comments. You never know who may receive or pass on something you thought would remain private.
- Respond to e-mails or ask to be removed from unwanted routing lists.

- Some companies can and will monitor employee e-mail. Legally, employers have the right to read all employee e-mail on their computer systems. Thirty-two percent of large U.S. companies pay people to read employee e-mails. According to Proofpoint Inc., 28 percent of large U.S. companies have terminated employees for e-mail policy violations.
- Don't let e-mail (or any other written form of communication) substitute for discussing important issues in person.
- If e-mailing internationally, keep the language as formal as possible. Casual language, clichés, jargon, and slang words or phrases may have different meanings elsewhere.
- Make sure you have a signature line at the end of your e-mail message. Quick reference to your full name, title, company, address, phone, fax, e-mail, and Web site will make it easy for people to contact you.
- If you are out of your office for an extended time, use the "Out of Office" tool so people sending you e-mails will know that you are not available to answer immediately. You can also provide information about your return, other ways to contact you if necessary, and any other details, but keep your message short and concise.

Technology has been driving us to reach new goals that are faster, more efficient, and instantaneous. But, with this technology, very few rules of business etiquette have come along with our training. We are taught how to beat the competition, think strategically, and get the best return on our investment, but we are not being taught the best method to get there.

Every day something new is on the market to improve the speed in which we conduct business. At this moment, the quickest and least expensive means to efficiently communicate our messages is through e-mail. But with all this efficiency comes a slight downside.

When should we use e-mail or some other form of electronic mechanism and what message does it convey to the receiver? Are you the one sitting in a meeting and texting a friend? Let's hope not.

At one time, there was only the mail. Yes, it is still there and for a very minimal fee we can still send a letter or document, but that may take a day or two, which is not acceptable. Then along came the fax. Not as pretty as receiving an original document, but nonetheless it was there within minutes instead of days. And now we have the e-mail and all other forms of electronically transmitting our messages. It has everything we could possibly need with an original copy in color with pictures and graphs and can be in the hands of the recipient, even across the world, in seconds.

But is it always the right and proper means of sending communication? Are we jeopardizing our people skills and the best way to communicate with one another just because we must be fast and outdo the competitor?

Even though our world keeps moving faster and faster and we struggle to keep up with all the technological changes, it is still unprofessional and offensive not to practice common courtesies and show respect for others. Let's hope we never get too fast.

RSVPs

RSVP is the initialism that people will see at the end of an invitation but many times will overlook. *RSVP* stands for the French phrase *Répondez s'il vous plaît,* which means to "please reply." The person who is sending the invitation wants you to accept or decline as quickly as possible. Even though a deadline for your response is generally listed, you should try and respond within three days to help the host plan for the correct amount of food and drink and space that will be needed.

When you do RSVP, make sure you are responding for only the people who were addressed on the envelope. Don't just decide to include your partner and all the kids in the neighborhood. Don't call to ask if you can bring a few "extras" to the event. Honor the person who is hosting this event and come with only those who were invited, arrive on time (with a gift in hand if necessary), and come properly dressed. Then you will probably be invited again.

Handshakes

There are many stories about the history and origin of the handshake, but most believe that this custom has several purposes that have evolved over the years. In years past, it could solidify an agreement; close a deal; seal a promise to lend or repay money; or act as a secret ritual for a fraternity, sorority, or secret society. Some say the reason for the right hand being extended was to make sure you were not going to grab for a concealed weapon and harm the other person. It is said that the shaking was added to make sure if there were any concealed weapons in the sleeve, the shaking would force them to fall to the ground or at least be exposed.

The handshake now is used more as a welcome or closing gesture, to provide a sense of equality and to level out the playing field, and to offer a sense of solidarity. The simple action of a face-to-face interaction and clasping hands can extend into friendliness, hospitality, and a level of trust.

Summary

Etiquette is crucial in all we do. You could spend years in school preparing for a career, days preparing for a board meeting, or hours working on a proposal only to have it all crumble right before you because of improper behavior. Manners are a critical part of the skills that people accomplish and learn over time. It does truly start at birth and gains momentum during those early childhood years. But, as time progresses, we become lazy and too busy to be considerate of others, to thank a coworker for a job well done, or to send our supervisor a handwritten note for considering us for a promotion. It's the little things that make the difference and separate you from the competition.

Questions and Answers: Seek and Ye Shall Find

Materials

Copies of the Question and Answer Cards cutouts (provided), prize for drawing

Time

15 to 30 minutes or the duration of the registration/reception time frame

Procedure

When participants arrive for check-in, give them either a Q card with a question or an A card with an answer. Let them know that there is a partner to their card. If they have a question card, then they will need to pursue the answer card or vice versa. (See Tips below for how to make this process easier.) Once they find their partner, they can turn in their cards along with a business card for a drawing. Make the drawing worthwhile to encourage participation.

Tips

• Color-code the cards so questions are one color and answers are another. You can use the company's logo colors, local school colors, or other choice that can show an easy difference between Q and A.

• If you have a large group, the Q and A cards can be duplicated more than once, but each participant needs to find only one partner.

Discussion Questions

1. Was it more difficult to find the correct partner than anticipated?

2. What are some other tips that are also useful in day-to-day people skills?

3. Even if you didn't find your match, were you able to meet three or four new people?

CUTOUTS

Question and Answer Cards

Directions

Copy and cut out the cards on this page. Hand each attendee a Q card with a question or an A card with an answer. Have them work the room introducing themselves, but trying to find their partner for this Q&A search. You can color-code the cards so it's easy for the attendees to find a different color.

Q:	What is the proper order of introductions?
A:	Higher rank, older, woman—HOW
Q:	How long does it take to make a first impression?
A:	3 to 5 seconds
Q:	When and how often should you state your phone number when leaving a message?
A:	Twice: once in the beginning of the message and again at the end
Q:	What does "3-3-3" represent?
A:	Thank-you notes take only 3 minutes to write, only 3 sentences are needed, and they should be sent in 3 days.
Q:	Who pays for the business meal?
A:	You invite, you pay.
Q:	If someone asks for just the salt, do you hand that person only the salt?
A:	No, salt and pepper are married and always travel together.
Q:	Name a few places a cell phone should not be used.
A:	Movie theaters, churches, funerals, restaurants, school zones, bathrooms, stores, drive-through windows

Q:	May I bring a guest if an invitation states only my name?
A:	No, never, what were you thinking?! And don't call to ask.
Q:	Where should name badges be placed?
A:	On the right side for easy reading. When shaking hands, your eyes follow your hand.
Q:	If someone just randomly presents you a gift, do you need to reciprocate?
A:	No, simply thank that person and follow up with a handwritten thank-you note.
Q:	How much should you tip on average at a full-service restaurant?
A:	15 to 20 percent is customary.
Q:	What is the most important part of an e-mail?
A:	The subject line
Q:	Where do you place your napkin if you leave the table for a brief time?
A:	On the seat of your chair or on the back of the chair
Q:	What should always match on a gentleman?
A:	His belt and shoes
Q:	What does RSVP stand for?
A:	*Répondez s'il vous plaît* (French for "Please reply")
Q:	If your meal is buffet style, what do you do with your plate if you would like to go back for seconds?
A:	Always leave your dirty plate at the table and get a clean one.
Q:	True or False: While dining, if unexpectedly you sneeze or cough you may use a handkerchief or your napkin. But, if you need to blow your nose or the coughing and sneezing persist, you need to excuse yourself from the table and move to a more private area or a restroom.
A:	True; if ongoing, then excuse yourself and go to the restroom.

The Napkin Game: How Many Uses Are There for a Napkin?

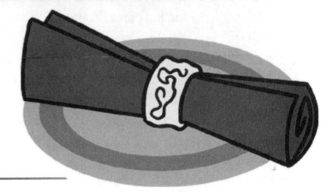

OBJECTIVES
- To learn how to properly use a napkin during a meal
- To work as a team to achieve the most creative napkin design

Materials

Two cloth napkins per participant (a clean third napkin will be provided for the meal), sample folds and displays for napkins, judges, prizes for winners

Time

15 to 30 minutes

Procedure

Attendees will be given two napkins as they enter the room or napkins can be placed at each table setting. Participants at each table will work as a team creating a design to enhance the table setting. Sample napkin designs or pictures of designs can be placed at each table for attendees to either duplicate or use as a basis for their design. The second napkin is to be used for them to wear. This can be headgear, a scarf, a bandanna, or any other creative design. The third napkin will then be placed by the wait staff for attendees to actually use during their meal. You definitely want to take away the napkin they were using to create their table design since more than one person might have handled it. Allow them to keep the napkin they are wearing throughout the meal. You can provide a basket or container at the door as they are leaving the room to deposit that napkin. Or, the company or association logo could be placed on that napkin (bandanna) as a takeaway.

Awards can be presented for the best overall table, best individual, best napkin design, and the best creative fashion style of a napkin. Once the contest is completed, go over the correct use of napkins during a meal.

Tips

- Make it fun by having some of the attendees display their new napkin design for the table and model their new clothing accessory.
- This game can be played as a team effort or each person can work separately.
- Napkin tips and information can be provided once the contest is completed. This could include:
  - Unrolling the napkin if silverware is placed inside the rolled napkin
  - Properly placing the napkin on their lap
  - Using the napkin throughout the meal
  - Where you should place your napkin if you leave the table during the meal
  - Where your napkin is placed at the end of the meal
  - Using the napkin as a tissue (bad!)
  - Never tucking your napkin inside the collar of your shirt or blouse

Information for Napkin Use

- Place the napkin on your lap as soon as you are seated or wait for your host to place his or her napkin first and then follow.
- Your napkin is not a flag to signal the start of a race, so do not flap it around.
- If the napkin is large, fold it in half or in the triangle fold.
- If silverware is rolled into the napkin on the table at your setting, take the entire napkin and place it on your lap and unroll it. Then place the silverware on the table in the correct positions.
- If you leave the table, place your napkin on the chair and gently push the chair back under the table. You can also place it on the back or arm of the chair.
- At the end of the meal and program, pick up the napkin from the center and loosely place it on the table. It will either be set to the left of your plate or, if your plate has been removed, may take the plate's position in the center.
- The napkin should stay on your lap until you actually get up to leave the dining area. If there is a speaker after your meal, the napkin should remain on your lap.
- Never use the napkin as a hanky or tissue. If you sneeze, you can blot, but don't blow your nose or rub your face.

- Don't wipe your mouth with one hand while holding a knife or fork with the other.

Discussion Questions

1. Were you aware of the proper way to use a napkin?
2. What were some of the things you were not aware of for proper use of a napkin during a meal?
3. What are one or two things that you were not doing properly and can now correct?

The Table Dining Game

Materials

Complete place settings for each team (see handout); team numbers for each person; corresponding table numbers for the teams; tables (skirted) for each team; bell, whistle, or horn for each team; chairs for each team player at table; copies of the Table Dining Game handout (provided) for the judges; judge(s); prizes for the winning team

Time

15 minutes once the game begins

Procedure

As they arrive and register, present participants with one or more pieces of their team's place setting along with their assigned team's number. You can determine in advance the number of items you would like to use, from an informal setting to a complete formal setting (see "Items for Place Setting" below). The attendees' place setting items will be a good basis for chit-chat during the reception. Everyone can compare items and try to figure out what they will be doing with them. They are also encouraged to find people throughout the reception who have the same team numbers.

Have cocktail or smaller tables with chairs set throughout the room with corresponding team numbers. The number of attendees will determine the number of tables. Try not to exceed eight to 10 people per team. Since each team is assembling only one place setting, more than that per table will be too crowded and the participants will lose interest. You can have even as few as two working as a team, but four to six is the ideal number.

At the end of the reception, all guests will be asked to proceed to their designated team's table. An emcee should announce that everyone has one or more pieces of a place setting and that they will work as teams to assemble a perfect table setting in the least amount of time.

Each table should be provided with some form of communication to announce they have finished this game. It could be a bell, whistle, horn, or just screaming. As soon as the team feels all is set properly, they must take a seat at the table and signal they have finished. All competition is stopped until a judge can check if all items are set properly (judges can refer to the handout). If so, that team wins. If the team's place setting is incorrect, the judge will only state there is an error and they need to figure out what needs to be changed. The signal is given for all to continue with the game until a team wins.

All members of the winning team could be presented gift cards from a fast-food restaurant (McDonald's, Arby's, Burger King, Wendy's), where none of these skills are necessarily needed. The handout could also be presented to all attendees at the conclusion of the game for future use and assistance.

Items for Place Setting

This setting has 23 items. However, you can easily eliminate some of the pieces (wine glasses, sherry glass, champagne glass, ice-tea spoon) or combine items (soup bowl and soup spoon, coffee cup and saucer, or all the forks, all the spoons, and all the knives) as they are presented to each attendee upon arrival. It depends on how formal you want to be and the number of attendees you have in the audience. Remember, each team is setting only one place setting, not the entire table.

- Entrée plate
- Soup bowl
- Soup spoon
- Bread-and-butter plate
- Coffee cup
- Coffee-cup saucer

- Water glass
- Ice-tea glass
- Wine glass
- Champagne glass
- Sherry glass
- Salad fork
- Entrée fork
- Fish fork
- Oyster fork (could determine the winner)
- Dessert fork
- Teaspoon
- Ice-tea spoon
- Dessert spoon
- Salad knife
- Steak knife
- Butter knife
- Napkin

Discussion Questions

1. Were you surprised that not all the teams completed the exercise properly?

2. With what part did your team have the most challenges?

3. Will you be comfortable now in any formal dining situation?

The Table Dining Game

Your table should be geometrically spaced to present a balanced appearance.

1. The service plate or charger plate is your starting point and placed in the center of the place setting. You will not eat from this plate; it is just used as an under plate. Different courses may be placed on top of it, but once the entrée is served it will be removed.

2. The napkin may be placed in the center of the charger plate or to the left.

3. The bread-and-butter plate is placed to the left of the place setting and above the forks.

4. Silverware is placed according to the way it will be used starting from the outside and working your way into the plate.

5. Forks will appear to the left of the plate and the knife and spoons to the right, with the knife being the closest to the plate. But there always is an exception. And that exception is the small fork used for eating oysters. This is placed to the right of the spoons. This is the only fork that will ever be placed on the right.

6. There can be as many as five glasses and in descending size order. Start with the water glass at the top and directly above the knives. The champagne flute is placed to the right with the red wine, white wine, and sherry glasses below these.

7. The rules of etiquette state that no more than three of any silverware be placed on the table at the same time. Again, the exception is that little oyster fork. Generally if more than three courses are presented before the dessert, they will provide the next utensil when the course is presented.

8. The dessert spoon and fork for a formal setting will be presented when the dessert is served. In an informal setting, the fork and spoon are placed horizontally above the charger or entrée plate.

Business and Dining Etiquette

Materials

Copies of the Business and Dining Etiquette handout (provided), pens or pencils

Time

15 to 25 minutes

Procedure

Etiquette can be fun and will make the difference in all we do. Each audience member or team will receive a copy of the handout. Explain that there are 27 words relating to business or dining etiquette hidden within this puzzle. The words can be found horizontally, vertically, and diagonally. Some letters may also be used more than once. To get the game started, you could show one of the answers from the puzzle.

Discussion Questions

1. What other words come to mind when you think of business and dining etiquette?
2. Are your skills polished or what new skills do you need?
3. Thinking of people who exemplify good manners and courtesies, what separates them from other coworkers or associates?

Business and Dining Etiquette

Directions

The words to search are related to people skills and business etiquette. Words can be hidden horizontally, vertically, or diagonally and may even cross over using the same letters.

Word List

Handshake	BlackBerry	Kindness	Introductions
Event	Casual	Etiquette	Dine
Email	Business Card	Text	Travel
RSVP	Voice	BandD*	Cell
Laptop	BMW*	Smile	Chat
Napkin	Appearance	Leader	Knife
Meet	Thank You	Protocol	

BandD represents "bread and drinks" and *BMW* stands for "bread, meal, and water." Both are helpful tips for correctly using the proper place settings for meals.

P	H	R	Y	R	R	E	B	K	C	A	L	B	A
B	A	N	D	D	T	H	A	N	K	Y	O	U	L
I	N	T	R	O	D	U	C	T	I	O	N	S	S
R	D	I	N	E	S	A	A	A	E	V	W	R	I	L
S	S	M	I	L	E	H	S	X	I	M	T	N	L
S	H	V	O	I	C	E	U	T	L	B	J	E	E
E	A	H	P	S	C	L	A	P	T	O	P	S	V
N	K	N	I	F	E	C	L	I	A	M	E	S	A
D	E	T	I	Q	U	E	T	T	E	E	L	C	R
N	A	P	K	I	N	L	E	A	D	E	R	A	T
I	E	V	E	N	T	L	O	C	O	T	O	R	P
K	A	P	P	E	A	R	A	N	C	E	F	D	E

Business and Dining Etiquette Answers

+	H	+	Y	R	R	E	B	K	C	A	L	B	+
B	A	N	D	D	T	H	A	N	K	Y	O	U	+
I	N	T	R	O	D	U	C	T	I	O	N	S	+
R	D	I	N	E	+	+	A	E	+	W	+	I	+
S	S	M	I	L	E	H	S	X	+	M	+	N	L
S	H	V	O	I	C	E	U	T	+	B	+	E	E
E	A	+	P	+	+	L	A	P	T	O	P	S	V
N	K	N	I	F	E	C	L	I	A	M	E	S	A
D	E	T	I	Q	U	E	T	T	E	E	+	C	R
N	A	P	K	I	N	L	E	A	D	E	R	A	T
I	E	V	E	N	T	L	O	C	O	T	O	R	P
K	A	P	P	E	A	R	A	N	C	E	+	D	+

9

Public Etiquette: Boats, Planes, and Automobiles

A journey of a thousand miles must begin with a single step.

—Lao Tzu

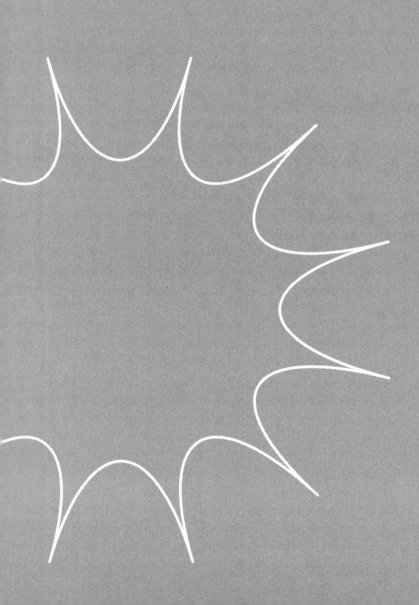

Every day you encounter public etiquette even if you do not realize it. Changing lanes in your car or allowing a person to edge into traffic in front of you, getting on and off elevators, walking through a door, and pulling up to a drive-through fast-food restaurant or bank teller should all warrant little acts of kindness and civility. But, unfortunately, they do not always get that needed attention or thought. It does make a difference.

People skills and the way you handle them can make the person behind you either very aggravated or maybe put a smile on his or her face.

Building Etiquette

- The doors open on the elevator and all you want to do is get off. But before you can even take your first step, a herd of people starts pushing toward you. Let the people exit the elevator before you try and get on. If there are elderly people or small children, let them on first and nicely hold the elevator doors back to allow them the time to get on comfortably.
- When you walk through a door, take a second to look behind you to see if there is someone else also ready to go through the door. Hold it and hopefully you will receive a nice smile and a thank you. This is much nicer than having it slam in the other person's face.

On the Road Again

- All cars nowadays have turn signals. Use them. Then remember to turn them off.
- Remember, in North America the left-hand lane on a highway is specified for faster-moving traffic and for passing. It is not meant for drivers

enjoying a leisurely Sunday drive or going below the speed limit. Use your turn signals to pass and then get back over to the right.

- This is not quite about driving, but it still applies. Be considerate to the drive-through workers. This could be to cash your checks at the bank, order fast food, or even pick up your prescriptions. No matter what the situation, don't be talking on the phone. It usually only takes a few minutes for the transaction, so give that employee the courtesy and attention that is needed and that they deserve.

- Do you remember the movie *Fried Green Tomatoes*? There is a scene in which Kathy Bates is getting ready to pull into a parking spot when some much younger girls come down the lane and pull straight in and take her spot. She then proceeds to hit their car. Her response is that she "is older and has better insurance." That might be an extreme response, but make sure the first person waiting for a parking spot gets the spot. If you are that person waiting, make sure you pull over enough so that other cars can pass you if the wait is long, and use your turn signal to mark your spot.

- Park legally. Don't pull into handicapped parking spots unless that applies to you or a person in your car and you have the proper stickers or tags. Don't pull into a no parking area just so you can run into a store for a minute. It is still illegal no matter the time frame.

Invited to Someone's Home

- Bring a gift and arrive on time. Don't arrive empty-handed at a dinner or a party. If it is with friends, then you can help with the food by bringing a dessert or appetizer. Or bring a small gift such as a bottle of wine or a candle or something else they would enjoy after the visit. Don't bring flowers or any gift that would cause them to stop and have to be away from their guests. Flowers the next day would be great.

Electronic Devices

- Cell phones . . . where do we begin? Be kind to your luncheon partner by not talking on the phone to someone else while you are dining. All you are telling that person is that the person on the phone is more important to you than he or she is. When you are in public on a cell phone, be aware of the "cell yell" and watch your conversations. Keep all your conversations PG as opposed to X-rated. Some topics should be kept for more private areas.

- BlackBerrys, iPhones, iPods, and any other handheld equipment are not meant to be used in a theater, in a church, at a person's home, at work, in meetings, or at school. The list can go on. Just respect the people around you. Observe the signs that ask you to turn them off, and be considerate of the people who really don't want to hear your conversations or see the screen on your device.

Airline, Airplane, and Airport

- **Going through security—be ready.** Don't wait until you are on top of the conveyor belt to start to get ready. If you have a laptop, take it out of the case and put it in a separate bin. Put some identification on the top of your laptop. A small sticky label with at least your name is advisable. Laptops are like black suitcases; they all look alike at the other end of the conveyor belt. Move away and slide your items to the end as quickly as possible from the conveyor belt when your items come off. Allow the people behind you the space and easy access to collect their items. Hopefully they will move along quickly, too.

- **Liquids and 311.** The Transportation Security Administration (TSA) has set the one-bag limit per traveler that you can bring on an airplane. 3-1-1 for carry-ons = 3.4 ounce (100 ml) bottle or less (by volume); 1 quart-size, clear, plastic, zip-top bag; 1 bag per passenger placed in screening bin. Be prepared and practice the 3-1-1 rule to ensure a faster and easier checkpoint experience. If in doubt, put your liquids in checked luggage. There are exceptions made for medications, baby formula and food, and breast milk.

- **Shoes.** In most cases, shoes still need to come off, so be ready. Slip-ons are much easier to travel in than laced shoes. Some airports even have booties you can slip on so your tootsies don't get too cold or dirty.

- **Sitting in the gate area waiting for your flight.** Most people need only one seat to sit down. Don't take one seat for you, one for your briefcase, and one for your meal. Share.

- **Getting on the plane.** Get to your row and move in. Do not block the aisle, and do not stop to put your luggage above seat 5C when you are sitting in seat 25C. That's their space, not yours, so go use your own. Remember again to share. The foot space under your seat in front of you is yours, but the overhead is a shared communal area.
- **Phones.** Turn your phone off when asked by the flight attendants. Do not scream when you are allowed to use them. Everyone throughout the plane does not need to know about your family vacation or at what gate your partner needs to meet you. Be considerate of the people around you. Cell phones and all technology have advanced beyond needing to scream into the phone. Avoid the "cell yell."
- **Laptops and games.** Remember, they do make noise. It can be annoying if you use your laptop or play noisy games the whole way to Europe. There is a sound control on the game or DVD players, so use them. Laptops do vibrate and could bounce the seat in front of you. Even though headsets are required for all electronic devices, people around you may not want to rock and roll to the bass of your music. Children need games and toys to keep them content and occupied during the flight, but do not make them the noisiest ones they own. Nice quiet games and toys work, too. Remember your headsets and save the $2 to $5 that airlines are now charging for theirs.
- **Snack trays and reclining.** When you hear those announcements that you are free to recline your seats and use your snack trays, just be gentle. You do not want to bounce around the person in front of you by quickly moving those trays up and down. Nor do you need to recline so fast or far that it is a tremendous inconvenience to the person behind you. Go back easy, and allow that person a few seconds to prepare for your trip into their lap.
- **Speaking of whiplash . . .** When you get out of your seat during the flight, use your armrest to push yourself up or to get back into your seat. Do not grab the back of the seat in front of you. When you use the back of their seat, you are pulling them back, possibly waking them up from a nice nap and even grabbing their hair. Painful experience.
- **Watch those bags on your shoulder.** When you are moving down the aisle getting on the plane, watch those bags you are carrying on your shoulder. It can be painful when you swing or turn and hit people

as you go by. Conversely, stay alert and prepared to move quickly when one is approaching your area. If you duck quickly, you might just miss the flying bag.

- **Overhead bins.** You do not have to run up and down the aisles assisting shorter or elderly people trying to put their bags in the overhead compartments. But, if you are right there, help them out. It moves things along, and can be your good deed for the day.
- **Wait your turn.** When it is time to exit the plane, wait your turn. Do not come rushing and pushing from the back to get a few people ahead. Exit seat-by-seat, row-by-row.

Littering

- Don't litter. There are trash bins everywhere. Just hang on to your trash a little longer and then dispose of it. This includes empty bottles, empty food bags, wrappers, and anything else people drop on the ground, throw out the window, or deposit in the park, probably just feet away from a trash bin. Don't be lazy—save our environment. Always recycle.

Dining

- Dining is definitely a public encounter. The key points are not talking with your mouth full, waiting for all to be served before digging in, taking small bites, and remembering that a buffet is not your last meal.

Thank You, Please, and Excuse Me

- These short little words can make all the difference and even change or soften a touchy situation. Just a smile or a wave and a nod will help.
- People appreciate receiving a thank-you note, and notes should be sent to thank people for a job well done, a meal, a gift, or something they did for you or your company. An e-mail thank-you can be sent initially and followed up with a handwritten note.

Summary

When in public, just be nice to the people around you. Certainly there are things that bug you that you see happening on a daily basis. It takes very little time and effort, but the kindness and civility that you extend to people around you can last a lifetime.

Public Etiquette: It Takes Only a Second

OBJECTIVE

- To make attendees aware of the value and importance of being kind and polite to people in public environments.

Materials

Copies of the Public Etiquette Match Game handout (provided), pens or pencils

Time

5 to 15 minutes

Procedure

Courtesies need to be continued when you move out of your office or home. Most of these kind gestures take only seconds but can have a nice lasting impression.

Distribute a copy of the handout to each attendee. Allow them to mix and match. Review the handout for further discussion.

Discussion Questions

1. What other common public courtesies do you practice on a regular basis?

2. What bothers you or is offensive in public?

3. Do you notice a change of personality in others when you commit a small act of kindness?

Public Etiquette Match Game

Match each phrase in the first column to the correct corresponding phrase in the second column in this proper public etiquette exercise.

1. Let them out first   Inside voice

2. Take them off   Make sure it is your turn

3. Turn them away   Sitting beside you or the one you are talking to on the phone

4. Take me there   Please wait

5. Hold it   Keep everyone dry

6. Use your turn signal   Unless going to the Kentucky Derby

7. Let them in   The elevator can't go anywhere

8. Who's more important?   Don't point

9. It's not your turn yet   Let them through

10. No need to talk louder   It may save you only a second

Public Etiquette Match Game Answers

1. **Let them out first.** When entering an elevator, allow everyone to exit before you try and enter. **The elevator can't go anywhere** until they exit.

2. **Take them off.** Take off your hat **unless going to the Kentucky Derby**.

3. **Turn them away.** Direct your umbrella from passersby so you **keep everyone dry**.

4. **Take me there. Don't point,** but try and walk people to their destination when they ask for help with directions.

5. **Hold it.** Hold a door for a person who might be coming up right behind you and **let them through**. Hopefully that person will say thank you!

6. **Use your turn signal.** When waiting for a parking spot, use your signal and **make sure it is your turn**.

7. **Let them in.** When driving, observe common courtesy and allow another driver into the lane. **It may save you only a second** to speed up and not let them in.

8. **Who's more important?** The person **sitting beside you or the one you are talking to on the phone**?

9. **It's not your turn yet,** so **please wait** and do not interrupt.

10. **No need to talk louder.** When using your mobile phone, continue to use your **inside voice** especially if you just landed and are sitting on the plane or are in a restaurant or any public area.

Airlines and Airports: Those Friendly Skies

Materials

Copies of the Airlines and Airports: Those Friendly Skies handout (provided), pens or pencils

Time

10 to 15 minutes

Procedure

Slogans are catchy and effective, but are you promoting and selling the best that you can to your market? Keeping that in mind, how well do your customers remember you? Do you need to change your tagline? Distribute the handout to all attendees and let them try their best to connect each airline with their slogan and then review the answers to see how well they did.

Discussion Questions

1. How many did you remember? Once you heard the correct answer, did it "ring a bell?"
2. How many slogans do you know, but not the product?
3. What is the best slogan you have ever heard over the years?

Airlines and Airports: Those Friendly Skies

Directions

Part of every airline is their advertising and slogans. How well do you remember these catchy phrases, old and new?

1. Who stated they were "the only way to fly"?
   a. Pan American
   b. Delta
   c. Western

2. What airline stated they were "the proud bird with the golden tail"?
   a. Continental
   b. US Airways
   c. Northwest

3. They let you know "you are now free to move about the country."
   a. American Airlines
   b. British Airways
   c. Southwest Airlines

4. Who was "the top banana in the west"?
   a. Midwest
   b. Pacific Southwest
   c. Hughes Airwest

5. Which airline states they are "something special in the air"?
   a. American Airlines
   b. Continental
   c. Aloha Airlines

6. Dustin Hoffman's character in *Rain Man* refused to fly unless he could fly on this airline because it "never crashes."

a. Virgin Atlantic

b. United Airlines

c. Qantas

7. They were "up, up, and away."

a. Air Italy

b. Air France

c. TWA

8. Which airline once had the slogan "We love to fly and it shows"?

a. Delta Air Lines

b. Southwest Airlines

c. United Airlines

9. What airline is the oldest in the world and known as "the reliable airline"?

a. Iberia

b. LAN Chile

c. KLM

10. This "businessman's airline" once served four continents.

a. SAS

b. TWA

c. KLM

11. "Fly the friendly skies" with this airline.

a. Lufthansa

b. United Airlines

c. Austrian Airlines

12. This airline "is ready when you are."

a. Spirit Airlines

b. Aeroflot

c. Delta Air Lines

Airlines and Airports: Those Friendly Skies Answers

1. c. Western

2. a. Continental

3. c. Southwest Airlines

4. c. Hughes Airwest

5. a. American Airlines

6. c. Qantas

7. c. TWA

8. a. Delta Air Lines

9. c. KLM

10. a. SAS

11. b. United Airlines

12. c. Delta Air Lines

Answer That Phone

Materials
Cell phones

Time
3 to 5 minutes

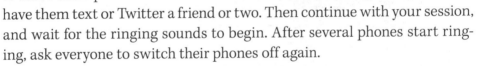

Procedure

At meetings and workshops, groups are typically asked to switch off their cell phones. Instead, try this: Ask them to leave their phones on! Then have them text or Twitter a friend or two. Then continue with your session, and wait for the ringing sounds to begin. After several phones start ringing, ask everyone to switch their phones off again.

Discussion Questions

1. What was your first reaction when you were asked to leave your phone on?

2. When the phones started ringing, did you have a hard time keeping your attention?

3. Who had the loudest (or most bizarre) ring?

4. When you sent your text messages or tweets, did you tell your friend where you were? What was your friend's reaction?

5. What are ways you can politely tell others to use better cell phone etiquette?

10

Leadership Skills

Management is doing things right. Leadership is doing the right things.

—Peter Drucker

There may be 50 ways to leave your lover, but according to Mr. Google, there are 511,826,667 (and counting!) links to leadership. So with all of this information to draw from, where does one start?

What exactly is "leadership?" What does it mean? What does it mean to you? What does it stand for? Most importantly, what do *you* stand for?

The goal of this chapter is to take a quick look at this multiplicity of meanings and to identify that leadership is really in the eyes of the beholder. In your role as a trainer, speaker, or meeting professional, you already know the answers. You've been leading your groups with a show of subtle leadership in your presentations, meetings, and training modules.

Leadership Defined

Let's start by looking at some of the experts who have written about this topic and see what they have to tell us.

For starters, take a look at this dictionary definition: "the art of influencing others in building trust and commitment . . . rallying people to a better future."

The acknowledged "guru" of leadership, Dr. Peter Drucker, said this: "The task of leadership is to create an alignment of strengths making our weaknesses irrelevant." And as you all would agree, a weakness is really nothing more than the absence of a strength.

Alignment—that's an interesting word. You've all heard the litany of management stories, e.g., the art of getting things done through others, whereas leadership suggests it's the art of getting the *right* things done through others. In other words, it's doing things right versus doing the right things.

Stephen Covey updates his *7 Habits* by now telling us that there's an eighth—"Find your voice and inspire others to find theirs."

Tom Peters in his book *In Search of Excellence* suggests that "leadership is a glorious adventure that marshals the talents of others."

Emotional quotient expert Daniel Goleman's book *Primal Leadership* sees it this way: "Great leadership works through the emotions. Our task is to 'prime' good feelings in those we lead."

Leadership author Warren Bennis writes that "character is the core competency of leadership."

Management Versus Leadership

As we compare and contrast the traits of leadership and management, you and your participants will quickly identify that the "leader" works with people and the "manager" works with things. Look at it this way:

The manager or COO

- administers,
- maintains,
- controls,
- does things right, and
- manages tasks.

On the other hand, the leader or CEO

- innovates,
- develops people,
- empowers,
- develops trust,
- does the right things, and
- leads!

So Who Are the Best Leaders?

A recent feature article in *Fast Company* magazine listed the top business leaders in the United States. The study, conducted by Harvard University, actually identified the top 100 leaders of the twentieth century as selected by more than 7,000 executives.

Here are the top 10:

1. Sam Walton
2. Walt Disney
3. Bill Gates
4. Henry Ford
5. J. P. Morgan
6. Alfred Sloan (General Motors)
7. Jack Welch (GE)
8. Ray Kroc (McDonald's)
9. William Hewlett and
10. David Packard (tie)

Flavor of the Month

As you reviewed the top 10 listing above, doubtless most of these are names readily known even a number of years later. What makes these leaders so memorable and what has been their legacy? Remember MBO (management by objectives), MBWA (management by walking around), 360-degree feedback, quality circles, and a host of other tools and techniques that caught the eyes of astute managers? Wherever and whenever we finds these "flavors of the month," we can always find disciples who claim to have found the "school solution" to whatever problem or crisis that may arise.

Clearly, some of these approaches have proven themselves over the years. As times change, so do management and leadership styles. In days gone by, management was defined simply as "getting things done through others." If that is the case, then leadership could be defined as "getting the *right* things done through others."

Summary

As stated previously, management means dealing with things whereas leadership means dealing with people. While it was once true that the leader got the respect of his or her employees simply by virtue of being the boss, in today's work world that won't fly! Managers and leaders must earn that right and it simply does not come with the territory. In a very real sense, leadership is defined not by position or power, but rather by practice and performance. And that, of course, is the central theme of this entire book—it's a "people business."

Leadership Is . . .

Materials

None needed

Time

15 to 30 minutes

Procedure

As you review for the group some of the definitions of leadership listed in the earlier part of this chapter, suggest that leadership is many things to many people. In teams of four or five, ask the group to think of some

people with whom they've worked or people that they know of who have shown great leadership abilities.

First, ask them to list a few of these traits individually and then get consensus from their teammates. Have them reach agreement on the single most important trait they feel is most critical for a good leader. (These will include such items as integrity, vision, listening, communication, character, and a host of others.)

Allow five to seven minutes for them to reach agreement, noting that this is a difficult decision. After each team has agreed on one item, they will identify this to the rest of the attendees and tell them why that trait is clearly the most important. They can do so by a skit, a song, or any other creative way to make their case.

Discussion Questions

1. What were some of the traits your team found to be common ones?
2. Who were some of the people—famous or not—that your group talked about?
3. Tell us about some characteristics you jotted down that were important but not necessarily viewed that way by others.
4. How difficult was it to reach consensus? Why?

Words That Relate to Leadership

OBJECTIVE
- To identify characteristics of role models and leaders

Materials

Copies of the Words That Relate to Leadership handout (provided), pens or pencils

Time

10 to 15 minutes

Procedure

There are many words and phrases that people will relate when they think of a leader. You want these words and actions to be a part of your daily activities and also your team.

Give each audience member a copy of the handout. Explain that the 20 words hidden within this puzzle about leadership can be found horizontally, vertically, and diagonally. Some letters may also be used more than once. To get the game started, you could show one of the answers from the puzzle.

Discussion Questions

1. What other words come to mind when you think of a leader?

2. When you think of yourself as a leader, what word or phrase best describes you?

3. What words from this puzzle do you need to add or work on for your own professionalism?

Words That Relate to Leadership

Directions

The words to search are about leadership. Words can be hidden horizontally, vertically, or diagonally and may even cross over using the same letters.

Word List

Change Agent	Integrity	Dedicated	Organize
Communication	Lead	Empowerment	Plan
Connect	Leadership	Enabler	Service
Courteous	Meet	Facilitator	Team Player
Creative	Motivator	Innovator	Trust

B	T	N	E	M	R	E	W	O	P	M	E	B	P
P	L	A	N	S	E	R	V	I	C	E	T	O	C
T	G	L	E	A	D	E	R	S	H	I	P	R	O
R	C	O	M	M	U	N	I	C	A	T	I	O	N
O	R	G	A	N	I	Z	E	M	N	O	L	T	N
T	E	N	A	B	L	E	R	E	G	F	A	S	E
A	A	D	E	D	I	C	A	T	E	D	S	U	C
V	T	R	E	Y	A	L	P	M	A	E	T	R	T
I	I	C	T	D	I	N	T	E	G	R	I	T	Y
T	V	E	A	C	O	U	R	T	E	O	U	S	N
O	E	E	R	O	T	A	V	O	N	N	I	M	L
M	L	O	F	A	C	I	L	I	T	A	T	O	R

Words That Relate to Leadership Answers

+	T	N	E	M	R	E	W	O	P	M	E	+	+
P	L	A	N	S	E	R	V	I	C	E	+	+	C
+	+	L	E	A	D	E	R	S	H	I	P	+	O
R	C	O	M	M	U	N	I	C	A	T	I	O	N
O	R	G	A	N	I	Z	E	+	N	+	+	T	N
T	E	N	A	B	L	E	R	+	G	+	+	S	E
A	A	D	E	D	I	C	A	T	E	D	+	U	C
V	T	R	E	Y	A	L	P	M	A	E	T	R	T
I	I	+	T	D	I	N	T	E	G	R	I	T	Y
T	V	E	A	C	O	U	R	T	E	O	U	S	+
O	E	E	R	O	T	A	V	O	N	N	I	+	+
M	L	+	F	A	C	I	L	I	T	A	T	O	R

Brain Teaser #4

Directions

Work with your team to decipher the hidden meaning of each box. See page ix for additional instructions.

1.	2.	3.	4.
#1+10	H S I W ——— STAR	CCCCNN	BUDDIES ITALIANS FARMERS
5. it's it's Time it's it's	6. APPLAUSE (in circle)	7. CHAWHORGE	8. ☆ $$$
9. SENTENC	10. 1derllsand	11. ing A	12. T N M N
13. 2hands 2hands 2hands ——— deck	14. 1111 ——— time	15. CLOUDY	16. fly_ng

Brain Teaser #4 Answers

1. First and ten

2. Wish up on a star

3. Four seasons

4. Friends, Romans, and countrymen

5. It's about time

6. A round of applause

7. Who is in charge?

8. Starbucks

9. Unfinished sentence

10. Alice in Wonderland

11. A huge following

12. Tiananmen Square

13. All hands on deck

14. For once upon a time

15. Partly cloudy

16. Flying blind

The Day After Tomorrow

Materials

Copies of the Day After Tomorrow handout (provided) or PowerPoint slide, pens or pencils

Time

10 to 15 minutes

Procedure

We seldom take time to think about our own future and how those "tomorrows" might look like for us. Ask each individual to look over the items shown on the handout and take a serious look as to how they see themselves a few years from now. Have them think in terms of these areas of their life and jot down privately what they'd like to be—or what they'd like to have accomplished in each area.

If the group feels comfortable sharing with one another, allow time to do so. If some would like to share their visions for the future, allow a few minutes for this.

Discussion Questions

1. How many of you have ever taken the time to do this kind of "blue sky" thinking?
2. How many of you identified some areas of your life you really hadn't thought that much about?
3. What are those areas that you might like our help with?
4. What do you plan on doing to start reaching those goals?

The Day After Tomorrow

Directions

We seldom take time to think about "tomorrow." As you review the items listed below, think about what you'd like to be or to have a few years from now. Jot down your comments alongside these areas—and add a few others not listed. Be as specific as you can.

Career:

Earnings:

Family:

Home:

Friends:

Education:

Health:

Social:

Personal skills:

Other:

Reprinted with permission: Adapted from *Time Management* program, Greenwich Institute

11

Managing Change

Become a student of change. It is the only thing that will remain constant.

—Anthony J. D'Angelo

In today's fast-paced and ever-accelerating days of change, it seems the only constant is indeed that of change itself. Unless one has been on a Rip Van Winkle sabbatical the past 20 years, it's pretty obvious that change is the name of the game.

This chapter will look at change—not from the technological perspective, but rather from the "people" point of view. In keeping with the theme of this entire book, we'll be addressing change from the human resources viewpoint. Clearly, there is no question that most of the changes we are experiencing have to do with new electronics, gadgets, and all the bells and whistles connected thereto. If you doubt that for even a millisecond, just check your desk or office. Many new methods of telecommunication are coming down the highway at warp speed. The rate of obsolescence of these devices is ever-increasing. Without question, last year's (or maybe even yesterday's) newest item is already old hat.

We'll be studying the process of change and delve into the psychology of change itself. And since, for many of our colleagues and attendees, there may be an inherent fear of change, we'll offer some ideas as to how these fears might be met and overcome.

Change Is . . .

Ask a few of your friends or audiences what change is and you may well get dozens of different answers. For the more experienced worker, it may bring about a negative response. Because of their longevity, they likely have experienced hundreds of changes on the job. And unfortunately, if their experience parallels that of other older workers, there may well be an inherent fear of any changes they'll be encountering. Perhaps they were "burned" by a former manager or supervisor and that memory will not fade away. Our task as speakers, trainers, and meeting planners is to supplant that negative image with a healthier one wherein change can be seen as a positive scenario.

In other words, change is all about people—and they may surprise you with their reactions to it. For the Gen Xers and the millennials in your programs, their response to change is often welcoming. They need variety and excitement, and Gen Xers may see change as that vehicle to provide it.

Remember that in introducing change—whether it is a new policy or a new IT system—the best surprise is no surprise! Let people know in advance of the impending change and even solicit their comments and ideas about it. By so doing, they are given an active part in the change and often will buy into it that much easier.

It is important to anticipate that there may be some resistance, but with advance notice and open and clear communication, this can be considerably lessened. And don't overlook the importance of informal communication in this process. In many cases, this informal network can work in your favor. Be honest and forthright and ensure that both the positive aspects and potential downsides of the change are brought forth.

The Three Rs of Change

1. **Resistance.** As already implied, there may well be some initial objection or resistance to the new policy or program. Whatever the case, this change can work in your favor if the individuals involved can see what's in it for them. Studies have shown that in instances where people can see how this change will benefit them—either in the long term or short term—they are more likely to help sell it.

   A quick activity may illustrate why change is often resisted. This is an "oldie" for most of you, but it still proves the point. Ask your participants to simply fold their arms in a manner that is comfortable for them. When they have done so, ask them not to look down but to quickly identify which arm is on top. After they respond, ask them to unfold their arms and refold them so that the other arm is on top.

   Ask them how they feel. Does it seem awkward? Uncomfortable? Weird? This often gets a laugh, but make sure they see the point. If indeed this physical change doesn't seem right, then how about psychological change?

   Read over these vintage quotes and you'll see that for many people, there has always been that mental block to new ideas:

- "There is no reason anyone would want a computer in their home." Ken Olsen, founder of Digital Equipment, 1977
- "Who the hell wants to hear actors talk?" Harry Warner, Warner Bros. Pictures, 1927
- "I have determined there is no market for talking pictures." Thomas Edison, 1926
- "The horseless carriage will never come into as common use as the bicycle." *Literary Digest,* 1899
- "You ain't goin' nowhere, son—you ought to go back to drivin' a truck." Jim Denny, Manager of the Grand Ole Opry, after Elvis Presley's first performance, 1954

Clearly there are dozens of reason why change might be resisted. These would include fear of the unknown, job security, past experiences, confusion, complacency, and habit, to name but a few.

2. **Resentment.** "Whose silly idea was this one?" "What's the reason for this stuff?" In addition to the innate resistance that may surface, it may be accompanied by some vocal and verbal resentment. While this is difficult to handle, take some comfort in knowing that the noisy overt reaction is actually better than the underlying covert response. With the vocal part, at least you know what you're dealing with and can take remedial action. With those feelings and negativity under the surface, it is important to give these naysayers some "airtime" in a safe environment so their comments can be heard.

3. **Revenge.** Obviously, this is the worst of the three. The "I'll get even with those so-and-so's" attitude is dangerous and destructive. Human nature being what it is, there have been many documented cases of individuals doing strange things just to "get even." These have taken the form of minor thefts (pens, pencils, office supplies) to more overt behaviors. With social media so prevalent and all too easy, there have been situations where people have posted—for the entire world to see—their negative and damaging statements.

As an overriding piece of advice, consider this: Force leads to resistance; listening leads to understanding. Try it—you'll see it works.

The Psychology of Change

Think of a recent example when the element of change may have been sprung on you with little if any advance notice. Perhaps it was a new policy or directive from headquarters, a new staffing change that involved your immediate supervisor or manager, or even as drastic a change as your own position being eliminated or outsourced.

As you read through these respective steps in the psychology of the change process, see if they don't resonate with your experience as you faced this impending new situation.

1. **Shock.** Typically, the first reaction may be one of disbelief or even shock—"This can't be true," "There must be some mistake," or "Don't they realize how long I've been here?" While it is true that these sentiments may not find their way into words, it nonetheless is a very typical first response—covertly or, in some cases, even overtly.
2. **Denial.** "This can't be happening to me," "Surely this was meant for someone else," and other such comments begin to surface. These thoughts may be internal but are still strong feelings of denial.
3. **Anger.** While the first two steps may have been concealed from all but your closest friends and colleagues, the sense of anger now raises its ugly head. "Whatever happened to loyalty?" one might ask. "Just you wait," one might muse. "I'll get even with those so-and-so's." This anger may take many forms. Unfortunately in today's society, workplace violence is becoming all too common. Although the anger phase is to be expected, it must be controlled. We need some kind of outlet to vent these feelings—sometimes we tend to take it out on family or friends who become the unwilling focus of our actions.
4. **Withdrawal.** At this stage, serious feelings of self-doubt and low self-esteem come into play. At this juncture, we may well need the assistance of a third party or counseling service. People sink to a dangerously low level in their own self-confidence. Words of encouragement and honest conversation may help buoy up the situation, and continued contact with these people can rebuild their lost sense of self-worth.

5. **Acceptance.** While it took only a minute or two to review these five steps, it may well take weeks or months or longer to actually go through them in real-life situations.

In one case involving one of the authors, a close friend working in Convention Services at a local hotel that he used for his university-sponsored conferences was unexpectedly terminated for no apparent reason. This person had been working at this same hotel for several years and received numerous letters of thanks and commendation for her work. So when her general manager walked into the Convention Services office on a late Friday afternoon, called her by her first name, and said, "Convention Services—as you know them—are no longer needed at this property and you need to leave by five o'clock this afternoon."

Can you imagine the shock? In a later conversation with the now-fired staff member, she commented that when her boss walked in, she recalls seeing his mouth move but could not believe what she was hearing.

In later conversations with this colleague, she seemed to be a "perfect storm" of these five steps. In actuality, it took several months before she finally came into the acceptance stage. But in the first few months, she became quite reclusive, would not even get dressed for the day, and essentially was a loner.

A few weeks later, she was asked to come into the author's office for a few hours a day to perhaps help out a bit. There was no pay involved, but it did give her a chance to leave her home and get back on the search for employment. By the time she reached the "acceptance" stage, it was some six months later.

The ABCs of Selling Change

Check out these three steps and you will find the task of having your colleagues have a more positive attitude toward agreement will materially be present.

A. **Awareness.** Let people know well in advance of an impending situation that will personally affect them. Of course, this is easier said than done. In today's fast-paced work world, it may well be that change comes down to you with no advance notice whatsoever. Check out the daily mergers and acquisitions in the news and you'll get the point. Stories abound like the scenario presented earlier. While it is true that the best surprise is no surprise, there are cases where this is simply not possible. However, in those cases where you do have some jurisdiction, let those affected have as much advance notice as you can. Let them know the situation—honestly and candidly—and you'll find a more receptive hearing. Let them know the whys and the wherefores of the new policy or staffing changes and perhaps even get their suggestions as to how to make these change more palatable.

B. **Benefits.** If the change is a new policy or procedure, advise them of the advantages or benefits of the change. Honestly tell them of the pros and cons of the change and again solicit their input. Studies have shown that if a person can see personal benefits, the selling job is that much easier.

C. **Change.** Just do it. If the new change has been properly communicated, giving advance notification to those involved and taking time for their input and suggestions, it can be implemented without too much resistance. This is not to say that there won't be any pockets of resistance, but for the majority, the feedback should be positive. Make sure to follow up with all involved as the new change is initiated and carried through. Continue to keep them involved in the entire process.

Summary

This chapter has identified the process of change and to suggest that people may not necessarily resist change as much as they resist *being* changed! Remember that most change involves people and that's where your job as trainer, speaker, and facilitator of meetings is most important, As we said in an earlier chapter, "We're in the people business" and that mandates our skillful handling of the overall change process.

Psychology of Change

OBJECTIVE
- To offer attendees a methodical look at the process of change and how these steps can be handled with others

Materials

PowerPoint slides or flip chart

Time

10 to 15 minutes

Procedure

Reread the "Psychology of Change" section found earlier in this chapter.

Using a PowerPoint or flip-chart presentation, walk the group through the five steps (shock, denial, anger, withdrawal, and acceptance). Acknowledge that while they can be talked about in just a few minutes, in real life, it may take weeks or even months for a person to go through the entire process.

Ask the group if they, or perhaps someone they know, have recently experienced a change. This could be a downsizing, a reorganization, or other changes in their work or personal life.

Divide the group into teams of four or five and ask them to discuss any such scenario. See if indeed these five steps may well have taken place. If appropriate, ask if anyone would care to share his or her experience.

Discussion Questions

1. Do many of you have friends or colleagues who had such an experience?
2. How long did it take them before they reached the "acceptance" stage?
3. For those of you who personally experienced this, what advice or suggestions would you have found helpful in the early stages?
4. How can you help others right now who are being impacted?

When I Was a Kid

OBJECTIVE
- To allow participants or coworkers to get to know one another a little better and discover some little-known facts about each other

Materials

None needed

Time

15 to 20 minutes

Procedure

Remind the group that our values and overall beliefs are often "cast in concrete" as children, and by the time we reach our teen years, these values are part of our overall belief system.

Form groups of three or four and have them tell each other something about their childhood days and what they wanted to be when they "grew up." For example, "When I was a kid, I wanted to be . . . [a rock star, a firefighter, a teacher, and so on]."

Ask them also to divulge why they had selected that particular job, such as "My mother was a teacher." In some cases, the job or career they have now may not even have been invented then, such as IT specialist, computer programmer, and so on. If that's the case, what made them change their minds? Allow 10 minutes for this discussion.

Discussion Questions

1. Did most of you recall what you wanted to be when you were a kid?
2. Would anyone care to tell us about their childhood dreams?
3. How did you pick your present job?
4. Who or what influenced you most along the way?

Those Were the Days

Materials

Paper, pens or pencils

Time

10 to 15 minutes

Procedure

Over time certain words and phrases come in and out of vogue. This activity will highlight some of these examples.

Form groups of five to seven—if possible, try and have a wide range of ages in each. If necessary, assign each group accordingly. Ask each individual to think back over the years and recall some of the people, phrases, or items that were commonplace in their earlier days (for example, eight-track tapes, Frank Sinatra, the Berlin Wall, leisure suits). Ask them to write down as many as they can think of. As each person reads two or three from their list to their group, see how many of the others in the group have any idea of what they're talking about! Perhaps others have a totally different understanding of those words or items.

Discussion Questions

1. How many items did you find that had meaning for all in your group?
2. How many of you identified some words or names that meant nothing—or perhaps even had different meanings?
3. What were some of the words or acronyms that are no longer used?
4. Can you think of some examples at work where these differences may have caused a breakdown in communication?

12

Presentation Skills

A speaker who does not strike oil in ten minutes should stop boring.

—Louis Nizer

It was a bitterly cold day in Washington, D. C., when William Henry Harrison, the ninth president of the United States, gave his inaugural address. It was the longest such speech in history at the time. Because of blizzard conditions and his refusal to wear a hat or overcoat, the new president caught pneumonia and died one month later. Now, the reason we relate this story to you is to let you know that this may be the only case in recorded history where death could have been caused by public speaking. Therefore, in spite of what you might have heard about public speaking— or the attendant fears connected thereto—relax. It's not going to kill you!

Granted, you have likely seen articles that show that speaking is the number one fear of most people. In fact, some such literature puts speaking ahead of even death. Perhaps that suggests that one might prefer to be in the coffin rather than deliver the eulogy! But as trainers, speakers, and meeting planners, we all know the importance of good presentation skills. We're not suggesting that we all must be polished orators, but it is important to have a working knowledge of and to practice these ideas.

The Parts of a Speech or Program

These steps are really quite simple and easy to follow. If you're new to the field of training or speaking, not to worry. Many full-time professional speakers would admit to still having butterflies or first-day jitters. We can't promise to eliminate them (nor do we want to), but one of the goals of this chapter is to help you to get those butterflies to fly in formation!

So let's get started.

1. **Preparation.** Don't be misled when you see seasoned speakers or trainers seemingly glide through their presentations with the greatest of ease. While their experience on the platform or in training rooms has brought them much experience and expertise, you can rest assured that they still spend time preparing for those tasks.

It's been said that the three most important parts of any presentation are (1) preparation, (2) preparation, and, of course, (3) preparation!

It's been further suggested that preparation makes up for a lack of talent. This preparation includes a lot more than merely making sure your PowerPoints are in order and the projector or other visuals are all set up. It includes checking the room setup, the fire exits, room temperature, and a host of other items. We'll be going into more detail later, but let it suffice now to understand that preparation is the first and most important step.

2. **Presenting.** Here comes the big day! You've done the proper planning, you've gone through all your checklists, and you're ready to roll. So let's review the three main ingredients of the presentation:

   a. **The opening.** It's been said you always should begin with a strong opening and finish with an even stronger closing. So where should you start? Perhaps with a joke or humorous anecdote? A challenging statement? A quick climate-setting activity?

   Any of these could be the right answer. If storytelling or relating funny stories is your strong suit, go for it. However, an opening joke is *not* a requirement, and if not told properly, it can do far more harm than good. So, if you do use humor, make sure it's relevant and timely. Be certain the point of the story ties in with your overall content. The story could bring rip-roaring laughter, but if it is not germane, forget it.

   Perhaps a challenging statement, for example, "Half of you may not be in the same job next year," will capture their attention. In many cases, this is extremely helpful in breaking one's preoccupation and may capture their attention. A caveat—be sure that the statement is not one that may turn your audience off in those first few seconds. Once they're not with you, they may be against you.

   One of the best ways to open is with some type of climate-setting activity. This could take the form of a 30-second meet-and-greet, a quick get-acquainted activity, or any of dozens of other exercises sprinkled throughout this book. Stay away from those well-worn clichés such as "Who here wants to make more money next year?" or "Raise your hands if you want to . . ."

A good piece of advice is to get people involved early on in your presentation, but do so with a purpose. Time today is far too precious to waste on a fun but irrelevant activity.

How about simply starting out by stating the purpose of your talk or training and what they can expect to learn from your time together?

b. **The body.** What's your message? Have you identified the three or four main points you'll be covering? People need to know what your program is all about, so make sure they are informed of your goals and objectives. While it is true that different generations have different learning styles, you can rest assured that they all want to play a part in their own learning activities.

Obviously, the body of the program carries the main subject matter and content of your message. Choose from a variety of methods, but remember that the old-fashioned lecture method may well be outdated for your audience. People—especially the Gen Xers and Gen Yers—do not want to be talked at. The era of the talking head is dead—or at least it should be.

Make sure your content is timely, relevant, and practical. Give them information that they can use—today or tomorrow. The more pragmatic, the more usable, the more new information, the better.

c. **The closing.** Tell them what you're going to tell them (the opening), tell them what you're telling them (the body), and finally tell them what you told them (the summary and close). Review the main points you covered and leave them with a closing comment or two. (Later on we'll be talking abut questions and answers. For now, take our advice—never end with a Q and A session. Trust us.)

3. **Participation.** You already know that learning is not a spectator sport. Today's audiences are for the most part younger, more highly educated, and much more sophisticated than their counterparts of even a few years ago. Therefore, the importance of audience involvement is well established. However, do not misunderstand this premise. We're not suggesting that every presentation must allow time for group participation. For example, in a 45-minute keynote presentation to a large group of a thousand faces, there may not be time for such an

exercise. And to further clarify, the problem is seldom to get the group talking—rather it is how to get them to be quiet!

But for a training program or facilitation, participation is a must. Not only do our attendees expect it, they almost demand it. The many books (including this one.) that offer such exercises cover most any topic or subject matter. Recent brain research tells us that we need to "shift gears" every five to seven minutes in the session so as to maintain the attention of the group. Start out with a quick get-acquainted activity (two to three minutes) and then sprinkle a few others throughout the session.

Suggestions

Here's a potpourri of additional tools and techniques that you will find helpful. Each of these has an integral role in your becoming an even more effective trainer or speaker.

1. **The audience.** In a corporate setting, an internal HRD professional already knows the group. For an outside speaker, here are some point to consider:
   a. **Who are they?** What is their background? Their experience? Age? What about why they're there? Are they a captive audience who were told they must attend your program? What about their needs? Their own objectives? What are some of the "hot buttons" that they deal with on a daily basis?
   b. **Their interests.** What are those items that are of most interest to them about the topic? Again, are they there to really learn or just to get out of work for a few hours?
   c. **Their expectations.** Hopefully, you've already told them the objectives of your program. But what about them? Take time to ensure that the goals you've outlined are indeed in sync with theirs. For smaller groups (up to 25) it is fairly easy to allot some time in identifying their own goals and expectations. In many corporate settings, there may well be some hidden agenda items. If these are legitimate and relevant to your program, can you ferret them out and allow some airtime for open discussion?

2. **Notes.** To use or not to use notes—that is the question. One school of thought would have us believe that we should never use notes as it might show a lack of preparation. On the other hand, the authors have no problem whatsoever with using notes and even letting the audience see that you are using them. Clearly you are not going to be reading from them but only using them as a guide in your presentation. Many speakers use index cards on which they may have their main points shown and an overall outline of the session to keep them on track.

3. **Visuals.** Typically about a third of your group will be visual learners and would like to see plenty of visuals in the program. On the other side of the coin, the "death by PowerPoint" syndrome is becoming more prevalent. Your comfort zone with technology will dictate the use of visuals. However, experienced speakers and trainers would suggest that some visuals be used.

4. **Questions and answers.** Lest we forget, allow us to expand on our caution to never end a program with a Q and A. We are not saying that questions should not be permitted, but simply not to end the session on that note. Experience has shown that oftentimes the proverbial question-and-answer segment may be nothing more than a forum for someone who perhaps has an ax to grind. At times, a question raised by one person may be of absolutely no interest to most of the group. So, if time permits, certainly allow some time toward the end of the session for a Q and A, but also allow the last four or five minutes for your recap and close.

   In handling questions, follow these hints:

   a. **Listen attentively to the question posed.** As you listen, jot down a point or two the questioner is raising. This is particularly important if the questioner has multiple parts to the question.

   b. **Repeat the question.** This lets those who could not hear it know what's being asked, but it also gives you a moment or two to think about how you might want to respond.

   c. **Respond.** Answer the question succinctly and politely. If the question is one to which you simply do not know the answer, admit it. Ask if someone in the audience might have a suggestion. If not, ask the questioner to stay after the session so you can get his or her e-mail and get back to him or her.

One final thought regarding questions: rather than take individual questions, ask the group at their tables or in small groups of four or five to pose questions among themselves. More times than not, a query raised by one can be answered by someone else in that group. If not, have each group agree on one question from them, and that question can be asked from the floor.

Summary

Armed with this information, you will be better prepared for your next speaking or training assignment. As was indicated, don't worry about having those butterflies—even the seasoned pro has them. Rather, keep your material audience centered, keep them engaged and involved, and those butterflies will surely be right back in formation.

Take Five!

Materials

None needed

Time

5 to 10 minutes

Note: This activity can be used before any scheduled break in a half-day or longer workshop.

Procedure

Before you give the attendees a break (midmorning, lunch, or midafter-noon), tell them they're going to "take five." Ask them to form into teams of five and they will have five minutes to discuss what they've learned so far in the program. Each team will report on at least one thing they picked up and how they can use it. Following this, they can take their break.

Discussion Questions

1. How many of you found at least one new idea you can use?

2. How many of you identified some items that weren't even discussed so far?

3. Was there pressure to contribute so you can get on with the break?

4. Did some of you hear things that you had already forgotten?

Unaccustomed As I Am . . .

OBJECTIVE
- To offer participants a chance to give an impromptu talk

Materials

A set of 3 x 5 cards with the key points of your content

Time

25 to 30 minutes

Procedure

Toward the end of the workshop or training program, tell the attendees that they will have a chance to practice what you preached. This can be used as an overall summary or recap of the content of your program or training module.

Pass out 3 × 5 cards containing key phrases from your program, such as "motivating others," "traits of a creative person," "handling price objections," or any other topics that you covered in your workshop.

Give them a moment or two to gather their thoughts and then ask who would like to volunteer to give a brief talk on that topic. If no one volunteers, ask someone you know would not be embarrassed to do so. The speaker should announce his or her topic and give a quick two- to three-minute mini-session on that subject. Once finished, that person then calls on the next, and so on as time allows.

Discussion Questions

1. When you looked at your card, was it easy to construct and organize your thoughts?

2. When you were thinking of what you were going to say, how did you control the butterflies?

3. Why are some people more spontaneous than others?

4. Did you find this technique a good way to help you recall and remember some of the items we discussed in the session?

When Is Your Birthday?

- A fun and easy way to get all participants to meet other attendees, react quickly, and work on their presentation skills

Materials

Stopwatch

Time

10 to 15 minutes

Procedure

Tell the attendees to line up from one end of the room to the other in chronological order by their birthdays—not by birth year, but by their birth month and day. Have a starting point for January and an ending point for the December birthdays. Set a time limit for the size of the group to accomplish this task. One to three minutes should be plenty. Hopefully they will move toward the area of their room for their month and start narrowing down from there according to dates. Encourage a lot of screaming and yelling to accomplish this job. Announce the minutes as they progress.

Once they are in the correct order, participants will step out of the line to introduce themselves. This would be their 30-second "elevator speech." The audience can applaud to support the speakers' presentation abilities.

Discussion Questions

1. How comfortable were you with your presentation?

2. What were some of the characteristics of the better presentations?

3. What were some of the biggest errors a person made within their 30 seconds?

4. How can we improve these skills?

The All-Star

Materials
   None needed
Time
   15 to 20 minutes

Procedure

Toward the end of the meeting, tell the attendees that they're going to help you name the "all-star" team for this organization or agency. You're not going to do this in the traditional sense of naming individuals, but rather by identifying the respective characteristics deemed as requisite in that respective job or position. For example, if it's a sales training program, you would ask them to list such things as product knowledge, sales skills, listening skills, and so forth.

   Initially, after identifying the overall topic, ask each person to list four or five skills that he or she deems as important to make the all-star team. Then, have each person pair up with a partner to compare and contrast their ideas.

   After two minutes for this, have each pair join another twosome for a group of four. They now must get agreement on their top five all-star skills. Each team then reports their results to the whole group.

Discussion Questions

1. How did the listing of your colleagues in your partnerships or small group compare to yours?

2. When you heard their listing, did you find some areas of disagreement? How did you get consensus?

3. Would these traits be somewhat true of any type of position in this field?

4. If these are traits that you aspire to, how can you get help in learning more about them?

13

Team Building

Coming together is a beginning, staying together is progress, and working together is success.

—Henry Ford

If there's any term that has seemingly overtaken the management and business literature these past few years, it has to be *teams* and *team building*. Indeed, for quite some time now, it would appear that this concept is the panacea for all that ails our organizations worldwide.

The importance of team building has been well documented over the past several years. It builds collegiality and harmony in the workplace and helps ensure that we can work both more productively and effectively. The acronym *TEAM*—together everyone accomplishes more—is a proven truism.

Characteristics of an Effective Team

In all likelihood, you've seen and worked with all types of groups in your role as a trainer and a speaker. Certainly, as in any type of activity or endeavor, the team members can "make or break" the effectiveness of any such group.

In its simplest form, a team could be defined as "a group of individuals working together toward a common goal." A less polite definition, perhaps from our agricultural friends, may say that a team is a "group of animals harnessed together." This would be more amusing if it were not the actual belief of some managers.

Let's focus in on some of the key ingredients or components that make for effective team players.

1. **Common goals.** First and foremost, we need people who have bought into and believe in the importance of the task at hand. Going back to the crude rural definition of *team* above, unless those animals are pulling in the same direction, there's not much chance of any kind of success. Be certain to allow ample time at the first few team meetings to ensure that there is indeed "buy-in" to the project or assignment.

Without such agreement at the very start, you may find dissonance and disagreements that can easily sabotage any future chance of team efficacy.

2. **Clarity of roles.** Make sure all team members clearly understand their particular roles and responsibilities and why their backgrounds and experiences made their involvement possible in the first place. There is always room for leaders and followers—indeed, at times these roles may be switched and changed again.

3. **Consensus.** This is not to imply that all team members must be in agreement on every step of every item every step of the way. Rather, most of the team should be okay with the respective decisions and actions of the group at that particular juncture. It does not mean that every single team member must be 100 percent in favor 100 percent of the time. It simply means that the decision made on this particular point is one in which each team member can feel comfortable with the rest of the team. Without question, healthy discussion and polite disagreement can make for better decisions. But also remember that it is imperative that we can "disagree agreeably." That is to say, allow each person to have a say and respect those opinions. In cases where their comments may be irrelevant or totally off base, acknowledge their comment and, if necessary, comment on their contribution—never on the individual.

4. **Care.** The old adage "People don't really care how much you know until they know how much you care" may seem old-fashioned and trite in today's bottom line–oriented companies and organizations. However, it is critical that sensitivity to others' feelings and behavior be respected. Whether dealing with a seasoned employee or the "new kid on the block," your recognition of mutual respect is paramount.

5. **Communication.** Keep people informed all the way, all the time. Another piece of timely advice: "What a person is not up on, they're down on." Even in cases where bad news, such as downsizings or reassignments, come into play, be open and honest with everyone. And here is where empathetic listening can be a real ally in all your efforts. Hear not only what is being said, but also listen to what is not being said. If a team has any hope of successful results, it mandates that everyone is up to speed on all team actions.

Several other factors come into play that can clearly impact the overall effectiveness of any team. For example, creativity and problem-solving ability clearly come into play. Interpersonal skills such as conflict resolution, consensus building, and trust are all essential ingredients. Seeing how an individual's actions can impact the overall effectivness of the entire team is a great learning experience.

The above listing is not meant to be all-inclusive. Your own experiences can doubtless add several more traits that are equally important. For example, the climate—culture, management support, and so on—can materially help or hinder your efforts. Without overall cooperation of all members, failure could be imminent. Commitment on the part of every team member is essential. In those cases where this is a conspicuous absence, it is time to find a new team member.

Team Building

There are different types of team building. There is the traditional "classroom" approach that might be used for strategic planning sessions. There is also an approach that involves the participants in some type of outdoor activity, sometimes referred to as "ropes courses" (although this term is far too delimiting). Other team-building activities include such things as "trust walks," constructing items with scarce materials, and myriad similar physical activities.

A major reason a company may choose to do team building is simply to get everyone to know their colleagues in a more informal atmosphere. They can then transfer these skills to their respective jobs and even take their organizations to the next level.

With the ever-increasing changes in the workforce, it is imperative that both older and newer employees "get on the bandwagon." For example, a Gen Xer brings totally different values and belief systems to the job than his or her more senior manager. By engaging in some team-building activities, the individuals can become more accepting and understanding of others' experiences. This transfer of training has been shown to be effective in changing behavior, thus making for a more cohesive and harmonious team. Even if team members are reticent to take part in these "fun and games," they can still benefit and learn new concepts they can use in everyday dealing with their fellow workers.

In choosing an appropriate activity, planners must first identify exactly what they see as their goal or purpose for any team-building exercise. If an outdoor activity is selected, make sure that adequate space is available. Consider also the profile of the group—age, gender, if they already know one another, and so forth. Obviously, for outdoor activities, the physical condition of the participants must be considered.

Summary

As was stated earlier, there are times when dissidence and dissonance are present in a team effort. If the group can get "buy-in" on a common goal, set a good climate, and even make it fun, experience has shown that caring and cooperation often result.

The role of a skilled facilitator is an important one. Keen observation of the individual team members provides great insight as to "where they're coming from." By asking thought-provoking questions and getting everyone involved in the responses, the team begins to build confidence and collaboration. Most importantly, the facilitator must debrief the activity and, with the help of the participants, clearly show how these activities can be transferred and used on the job.

To create effective teams, management must first of all get involved. Team building is *not* a "spectator sport." Following the program, it is imperative that supervisors and managers continue to be supportive and refresh that camaraderie displayed during the activity. In addition to having a common goal, such items as clarity of roles, compassion, and climate are important. Mutual respect, recognition, and appreciation for others are all critical for an organization's success.

On the other hand, you really can't legislate team building. In other words, "Poof, you're a team!" just doesn't fly with today's workforce. You've already learned that leadership is based more on performance than on position. And clearly that's what team building is all about.

Sailing the Seven Cs

Materials
Paper, pens or pencils

Time
20 to 25 minutes

Procedure

Ask how many of the group are currently (or have previously) worked in a team, as either a team leader or a team member.

Ask the group to split into teams of three or four and to discuss among themselves what factors they consider to be imperative for an effective team to function. Although some of the group may not have firsthand experience in teamwork, it doesn't matter. Even the novice worker can identify some of these factors.

Tell them you'd like them to think of as many of these factors as they can, but to make it more interesting, suggest that they focus in on those words that begin with the letter *c*. These could include *clarity, communication, cohesiveness, care,* and so forth. Stress that there are no wrong answers, so they should try and get as many items as they can think of—all beginning with *c*. Each team should come up with at least seven *c*'s.

Tell them they will have five minutes to compile their list and then they must get consensus on what they believe are the top three items. Each team will then give a two- to three-minute presentation on their findings.

Discussion Questions

1. Which team got the most items?

2. Did you find it helpful (or not) to concentrate on only the letter *c*?

3. What were some of the more creative items you discussed?

4. Are there any examples you can share from your own workplace teams?

5. How would these items differ for those of you working in virtual teams?

The Price Is Right

Materials

Office-related items on display for bidding, four bins containing the names of the four teams' players, wheel to spin to select the two finalists for the grand prize (all contestants will spin and the two with the number closest to $1 on the wheel will make it to the final bid and grand prize), T-shirts or fun items (like buttons) for the audience and contestants to wear, buzzers and music to carry out the theme, emcee (similar to Drew Carey), prizes for winners

Time

30 to 40 minutes

Procedure

This activity will provide a better understanding of the monies spent for items from office supplies and equipment to attendance at a conference or seminar. Divide the attendees into four teams so they can support one another. This is a great opportunity to mix the various departments and areas from your company.

Have the emcee call the first four contestants (one from each team) to "come on down" from the audience. This can be done by pulling names from four bins. Once the four contestants have been announced, the first item comes up for bid. The four contestants give their bids after which the host announces the actual retail price. The person closest to this amount without going over comes up to the stage. Similar games and rules from the television show *The Price Is Right* can be used with items or events from your company. Provide various fun items for the contestants and their teams to win.

Once the first bid and game is played and completed, the next four contestants are called from the audience to "come on down." You always want to have one representative from each team. The end result could have all the winners being from the same team.

Prizes could be given to the final winning team.

Suggestions for Bidding Items

The purpose is for the employees to understand the value and monies spent throughout the year by the company. They will play and bid on these items and guess the correct amounts.

- Sales trips that are taken throughout the year by employees
- Office picnic held each year
- Annual holiday party
- Redecorating the offices
- New office equipment from pens to computers

Discussion Questions

1. Were you aware of the monies spent for the programs or equipment?

2. How will this alter your future spending?

3. How can you budget to bring these costs down?

Brain Teaser #5

Directions

Work with your team to decipher the hidden meaning of each box. See page ix for additional instructions.

1. famallily	2. $\dfrac{MD}{Call}$	3. E K A W @6:45	4. OBJ4ECT

5.
K
A
E
P
S
	6.
	In
	    for
	mat
	      ion
		7.
		
		BBBBBBBBBBBBBB
			8.
			
			$\underline{PURCHASE}$

9. MA✔IL	10. $\dfrac{COMPLETE}{HAUL}$	11. 1@3:46	12. M A R K E D
13. T E G DA WN	14. SHOºULDER	15. e b u n a D	16. COTAXABLEME

Brain Teaser #5 Answers

1. All in the family

2. Doctor on call

3. Wake up at 6:45

4. Foreign object

5. Speak up

6. Information gap

7. A swarm of bees

8. Purchase online

9. The check is in the mail

10. Complete overhaul

11. One at a time

12. Marked down

13. Get up at dawn

14. Cold shoulder

15. Up the river

16. Taxable income

14

Creative Problem Solving

If you can dream it, you can do it!

—Walt Disney

Ever find yourself in a rut? Does every program seem to be done the same old way?

This chapter will help clear away those cobwebs and flick on your green light for innovation and creativity. You'll learn ways to get your attendees involved and not be passive listeners. We'll identify just what creativity and innovation are and how you can assist your participants and colleagues to be more ready to try out and accept new ideas. You will learn the traits of creativity and see how these are common everyday items we all possess. You'll also review Walt Disney's "four Cs of creativity" and how these, too, can be incorporated into your own innovative efforts.

Definitions of Creativity and Innovation

Since we all may have our own way of looking at this thing called "creativity," let's see if we can find some common ground. A good place to start is with the dictionary, which states "to bring into being from nothing; to cause to be; to beget." In addition, it is "to be inventive; to be original."

Expanding on these words, creativity might be looked at as seeing things that already exist, but from a different perspective. Mike Vance, former dean of Disney University, put it this way: "Creativity is taking of the old and putting things together in new and different ways." Buckminster Fuller, who designed and created the first geodesic dome, said this: "Creativity is the miracle of the obvious. The only way to increase creativity is to just do it."

Thomas Edison spoke of genius in any endeavor by suggesting that it was 1 percent inspiration and 99 percent perspiration. One might paraphrase that by suggesting that ideas are funny things—they don't work unless you do!

John Naisbitt of *Megatrends* fame wrote that "an organization's main competitive advantage is that of creativity. More esoterically, we've seen it defined as the manifestation of the subconscious. Innovation can be looked at as the successful application of creative thought."

Studies in Creativity

Over the past several years, there have been numerous investigations about this fascinating field. The adage "You can't teach an old dog new tricks" is outdated. For example, Colonel Sanders started his first Kentucky Fried Chicken at the age of 65. Grandma Moses reached her fame as an artist when she was 78. Nelson Mandela, at age 75, received the Nobel Peace Prize. Walt Disney was in his early 50s when, after a number of failures, he finally saw his dream for Disneyland come to life.

As these examples illustrate, there is really no correlation between one's chronological age and one's propensity for being creative.

In similar manner, the relationship between one's IQ or intelligence is also nonexistent. In fact, the opposite may well be true. Consider this: by the time a person completes a college degree, he or she will have taken well over 2,500 tests, quizzes, and examinations—all with only one correct answer! Sad, but true. But we all know that there is always a better way of doing things. As a matter of fact, one good approach to being creative is to find out what everyone else is doing and then doing something different.

One important point that needs clarification: many authors and speakers tell us that we use only about 10 percent of our creative abilities. This makes for good reading, but that unfortunately is simply not true. Recent research shows that this is clearly not the case. However, for years and years, we have heard this myth being propagated. While there have been studies that illustrate that youngsters of five or six years of age use about 90 percent of their brain, this diminishes to about 20 percent when they get to school.

"Remember, Johnnie, make sure you color within the lines." Sound familiar? Well, Johnnie and Joanie and thousands of their classmates did exactly as told and we wonder why their creativity went downhill. Now, when we're told to get out of the box, we can start those creative juices flowing again.

A word regarding one's intelligence and the propensity for innovation and creativity. While one would like to argue that it is obvious that the "smarter" a person is, or the higher IQ he or she has, this is simply not true. As a matter of fact, there are compelling arguments that state exactly the opposite! Think about that for moment: there is no correlation whatsoever between one's "book learning" and one's ability to think creatively.

Refer back to our comment about Johnnie being told to color between the lines—not exactly the best way to encourage one's creative juices.

Traits of Creativity

So then, what *does* make for a creative person? What are some of the qualities or characteristics that distinguish the innovator from the others?

Studies at major universities the past several years seem to identify a handful of traits in a creative person. Check these out:

1. **Observation.** Yogi Berra, the famous baseball player turned philosopher, tells us that "you can observe a lot just by watching." That's pretty hard to argue with, but really now, how observant are we? When teaching creativity and identifying this first trait, ask your participants how observant they think they are. Ask them to close their eyes for a moment and describe the clothes of the person seated to their left or right. This usually gets a laugh since many of them cannot do so. Follow this up with the question, "Okay, then, can you describe your own appearance?"

2. **Flexibility.** Too many of us have "hardening of the categories." We tend to put ourselves in boxes and never get out. In problem solving, think of all the possible solutions and try them out. Being able to bend and flex with the situation and always looking for that better way is critical.

3. **Synthesis.** Sure, two plus two equals four. But what are some other possible answers? Being able to put things together and seeing different ways to approach them is part of this trait. It's the art of combining different scenarios and coming up with a consensus or combination.

4. **Originality.** This is perhaps the most obvious of the traits discussed thus far, but check it out. How original are we? We see others who are described as having "mental arthritis," or never having an original thought. Emerson told us that "the ability to create is the ability to adapt." So take that idea and play with it. What are some possible variations that can make it even more original and usable? Don't get sick with mental arthritis!

5. **Perception.** This picture has been around for well over a hundred years and is still a classic in many psychology books. Although most of your participants will have seen this, you'll still find a few who have not. Ask them which they see first: the old lady or the young woman. The adage that "perception is reality" is indeed a correct one.

Disney's Four Cs of Creativity

Few would not agree that Walt Disney was one of the most innovative and creative minds ever. His ideas for creating a theme park came to him one Sunday afternoon in Southern California after watching his two young daughters on the carousel, going round and round. "There's got to be a better way," he thought, and after a number of setbacks, his dream was realized.

Here's Walt Disney's approach to creativity:

1. **Confidence.** You need an air of self-confidence about yourself and your ideas. There will always be colleagues who will be quick to point out that your ideas have flaws and drawbacks. Listen to them—and perhaps even change or improve your idea—then drive on.
2. **Curiosity.** Ask not just "Why?" but more importantly "Why not?" What's the reason we've always done it that way? With new technology, can't we try something new and different? Ask the basic questions and strive for that better idea.
3. **Constancy.** Stay the course! Don't let the naysayers sabotage your innovative abilities. Keep moving in the right direction.
4. **Courage.** An old adage says, "Behold the turtle—he makes progress only when he sticks his head out." Sure, there will be times when you begin to doubt your own thoughts, but believe in yourself and take that risk.

Questions About Questions

As you review these ideas, think about how you can make use of them for your next training program, presentation, or meeting. Although this is not an all-inclusive listing, it does give you a good start as you generate even more new ideas. It starts with the ever-famous five Ws and adds a few other questions just for good measure.

1. **Who.** Who could help me move this idea forward? Who are the people I really need to "sell" this idea to? Who is most likely to benefit? Who can identify other methods to implement this change?
2. **What.** What is the first step I need to take to push this through? What are some potential roadblocks or barriers I must consider? What's my best selling point? What's in it for them?
3. **Where.** Where's the best place to send out a "trial balloon"? Where in the organization am I likely to face the most opposition? Where are my closest friends to help me sell this program?
4. **When.** When should I start? When is the best time to check out the idea? When should I confide in others?
5. **Why.** Why would anyone really want to buy in? Why didn't someone try this before? Why is this so important to me or my organization?

Brainstorming

An "oldie but goodie," this novel form of creative thinking first came to light years ago when Alex Osborne, an advertising executive, used it to generate more ideas from his employees. It worked then and, with proper instructions, will still work today. In far too many organizations, creativity is stifled because of the corporate culture or climate. By using the brainstorming approach, an open and clear channel is opened for anyone's ideas, from brand-new to seasoned staff.

The rules are simple and straightforward:

1. **No criticism.** Wow, what a concept! Doubtless, you've experienced the situation where you proposed what you thought was a really hot idea only to have your boss or colleague throw cold water on it. As

an analogy, if you turn on the hot water faucet and then mix in cold water, the result is lukewarm water. Keep the idea a hot one! In this step, no one is to offer critical judgment as to why it won't work. Keep all the ideas positive ones.

2. **The wilder, the better.** When was the last time you heard anyone suggest this? In these days of tight schedules and bottom-line meetings, who has the time to be free and open? We feel a need to stay with the company culture, and all ideas must be tested and proven. No way, says this principle. Let your mind roam and do your share of free-wheeling. Don't constrain yourselves with the "we tried that before" syndrome. Try something different.

3. **The more, the merrier.** Quantity, not quality is the desired outcome. The best way to get a good idea is to get a whole lot of ideas. Again, don't be hesitant to bring forth an idea because it might sound far-out. In actual practice, sometimes the seemingly crazy idea works out to be the best one. Let your mind be open and bring all those ideas to the table.

4. **"Hitchhiking" is welcomed.** Remember the time someone made a suggestion and you quickly thought of a way to make it even better? But rather than interrupt, you waited until later and then forgot the idea. In this precept, we're suggesting that it's perfectly okay to jump in even when you don't have the floor.

A word of caution: since these "rules" run counter to what many people see as decorum and etiquette in meeting behavior, you would be well advised to do a "trial run" on a hypothetical item before tackling a real-world issue. The best way to get people not familiar with this method acclimated is to suggest a quick one-minute exercise to get them accustomed to this open-air approach. As an example, have them form teams of three or four and, after explaining the rules for brainstorming, tell them they have 60 seconds to think up as many ideas as they can for the use of a regular paper clip. Ask someone in the group not to write out their ideas, but simply to keep track of how many ideas their group generated.

Summary

This chapter proves that creativity is everywhere. It does not belong only to the "rich and famous" but rather to everyone. All too often, your attendees may be working in a situation where their innovative and creative abilities are stifled.

By showing them that we all possess the basic qualities and characteristics of the creative person, their own abilities may flourish. So push aside those cobwebs and flick on that green light for creativity. And you'll even have fun in the process.

The Alphabet Game

- To be used as a "filler," for a change of pace, or simply for fun

Materials

Items that the participants have on hand or close by, watch or stopwatch

Time

5 to 10 minutes

A B C D E F G
H I J K L M N O
P Q R S T U V W
X Y Z

Procedure

Note: This activity can also be used in half-day or longer programs. As an example, if the entire group is not back at the 1 P.M. start time after the lunch break, use this as a "reward" for those back on time.

Tell the group they will engage in a timed activity to test their creativity and to see how they work under a sense of subtle pressure. They'll be engaged in a contest as simple as knowing their ABCs.

Ask participants to stand and form teams of four or five. (If they are seated at tables of five to seven, they form one team. If eight or more, divide into two teams). They must have—or find—an item that corresponds to each letter of the alphabet, starting with A, then B, and so on. They cannot skip letters. Before you say "go," tell them they have two minutes to get as far as they can through the alphabet and place each item on the table (or chair). For example, A could be an apple; B could be a book, C might be candy, and so forth. Call time after two minutes.

Discussion Questions

1. Which team got the furthest in the alphabet?

2. What were some of the more creative items that you found?

3. What were a few ways you found to be inventive, such as perhaps placing a chair (for C) on the table?

4. Did any of you take a moment and strategize first rather than jumping right in?

Are You Ready for Some Football?

Materials

Copies of Are You Ready for Some Football? handout (provided) or a PowerPoint slide, pens or pencils

Time

5 to 10 minutes

Procedure

Here's a fun game for sports fans. Pass out copies of the handout to each attendee or prepare a PowerPoint based on the handout. Tell participants that each of the clues represents a professional football team. They should first determine the team names (such as the Cowboys or the Steelers) and then identify each team's city, state, or region.

Note: Depending on the demographics of your group, this game may not be suitable for all ages.

Are You Ready for Some Football?

Directions

Here's a fun game for sports fans. Each of the items below represents a professional football team. Decipher the clues to determine each team's name (such as the Cowboys or the Steelers) and then identify each team's city, state, or region.

1. Sunbelt redbirds

2. 2 squared; three squared

3. King of the jungle

4. People with no clothes

5. Holy men and women

6. Accounts payable

7. Rich slick Middle Easterners

8. Six rulers

9. Former young ladies

10. Barbie's swim gear

11. Highest Boy Scouts

12. Lousy-spelling robbers

13. _____-setters

14. Wigwam patriarch

15. Ocean fowl

16. Army small insects

17. Six-shooters

18. _____ of the Lost Ark

19. Corn for $1 each

20. Credit card users

Are You Ready for Some Football? Answers

1. Arizona Cardinals

2. San Francisco 49ers

3. Detroit Lions

4. Chicago Bears

5. New Orleans Saints

6. Buffalo Bills

7. Houston Oilers

8. Minnesota Vikings

9. Cincinnati Bengals

10. Miami Dolphins

11. Philadelphia Eagles

12. Pittsburgh Steelers

13. New York Jets

14. Kansas City Chiefs

15. Seattle Seahawks

16. New York Giants

17. Indianapolis Colts

18. Oakland Raiders

19. Tampa Bay Buccaneers

20. San Diego Chargers

Brain Teaser #6

Directions

Decipher the hidden meaning of each box (which represents a TV show, movie, or entertainer). See page ix for additional instructions.

It's Showtime

Each of the frames represents a TV show, movie, or a well-known personality.

1. SWAP or SWAP (circled, crossed out)	2. IAMDERIOCL	3. inexperienced 5,280 ft.	4. OBRCONIEN
5. NOON	6. 2.5 MALES	7. **BOARD** JUNGLE	8. LEBOSTGAL
9. SMALL HOME ―――――― FARMLAND	10. NUDGED ACHERUB	11. RASINGINN	12. COST $ 1 0 0
13.　　**N** **W**　　　　**E** I N G　　**S**	14. SNOOZE —Seatintle	15. S(9-n)feld	16. Evening@MUZM

Brain Teaser #6 Answers

1. Deal or No Deal

2. American Idol

3. The Green Mile

4. Conan O'Brien

5. High Noon

6. Two and a Half Men

7. Blackboard Jungle

8. Boston Legal

9. Little House on the Prairie

10. Touched by an Angel

11. Singin' in the Rain

12. The Price Is Right

13. West Wing

14. Sleepless in Seattle

15. Seinfeld

16. Night at the Museum

15

Working with Difficult People

Holding on to anger is like grasping a hot coal with the intent of throwing it at someone else; you are the one who gets burned.

—*Buddha*

One would think when you graduate from high school that all the bullies would stay behind those ivy walls. But, to tell you the truth, they have only just begun.

Bullies come in all sizes, shapes, and ages, but now we change the word bully to the "difficult person" in the workplace. They can be disguised as the micromanaging boss, the temperamental or insecure coworker, the one who must always have the last word (be it right or wrong), the one who never agrees with anything the team presents, the always correct one, the "why can't you do it my way, it has always been done that way before?" person, the constant interrupter, the "fibber," the needs-constant-praise person, and the conflict creator.

Times change. Back in elementary school or high school, you could always send the bully to the principal, but what happens now if you are the "principal" or the manager of a company or the head of a department? You have to deal with this person.

But not all difficult people are bullies. Difficult people are also the ones who are indecisive (or the opposite and always agree with everything everyone says—the "yes" people), the "can't make up their mind" employees, the "know it all" employees, the gossipers, the complainers, and the ones who are negative toward everything—the "oh woe is me" employees. So, difficult employees have many moods, many traits, and many difficult and different personalities.

Conflict

According to the dictionary, conflict is defined as "a war; a clash between hostile or opposing elements or ideas; to show antagonism or irreconcilability." All that sounds pretty threatening and harsh. But some other words that are related to conflict include bothersome, troublesome, rigid, distracting, tiring, and unyielding. Unfortunately, that does seem to apply to some of the employees in our workplace. So, how do you deal with these "difficult" people in our workplace?

People Skills

Of course, it would be great to tell the difficult employees they will receive all new people skills and be the role-model workers of your company. But, unfortunately, it is not that easy. People can be trained, but to acquire a new attitude and a pleasing personality is a lot tougher. You can't necessarily change or eliminate their conflict, but you can create a way to handle it constructively.

Why Are People Difficult to Work With?

There are endless reasons why people react the way they do. A lot may even be related to childhood stress or problems, or some can be credited to more recent problems. The difficult employees could feel threatened or unappreciated; they could have stress from home or a personal relationship, a reputation as a bully that feel they need to continue, or the attitude that they are always right; or they could have just done it for so long and have always gotten away with it. The list could go on and on why people act the way they do, but how can you work with them?

Difficult Workers and Their Traits

- **Bullies or Bullyesses**
  - These are the "in your face" abrupt and abusive combaters.
  - Their temper has a very short fuse.
  - Employees are literally afraid to approach them or work with them on a team.
  - They are very confident in their decisions, so don't question them.
- **The Know-It-Alls**
  - No matter what you say or do, they already know it or they know something better.

- They are generally very productive and intelligent people. So, again, they think they are always right.
- **The "Yes" People**
  - They will always agree or tell you yes, but they don't always deliver or follow through.
  - They need your approval and want to be your friend.
  - You need to be careful if you are counting on this person to get things done.
- **The Snippy Ones**
  - They are a cross between the Know-It-All and the Bully.
  - At times they can be your best employee but then talk about you behind your back.
  - They complain constantly.
  - They can be very knowledgeable, know all the rules, live by the rules, but just have a bad attitude toward everything.
  - If they didn't complain all the time, you might listen to them because their complaints might have some value.
- **The Pessimists**
  - The Pessimists are worse than the Snippy Ones.
  - They are very negative and bitter.
  - They are bad employees for the morale of your team or company.
  - They never look for the solutions, just the rainbow for their pot of gold.
- **The Indecisive People**
  - They are hard to get an answer from or involved in projects.
  - They never share their thoughts or feelings.
  - They could be good employees, but it's hard to tell what they know or are feeling.
- **The Procrastinators**
  - They're worried they can't make the correct decision for fear of hurting someone.
  - They want to help everyone but never jump in to make a decision.
  - They stress out the team because they can't decide.
  - Once a decision is made and the goals are set, they are with you 100 percent.

- **The Tolerables**
  - They know their job and they know that they know their job.
  - They are so excellent in what they do that you overlook their faults.
  - They can be upsetting to clients and customers, but they do such a great job for them it is overlooked or even ignored.
  - They experience tolerable acceptance by other employees.

So, what do you do with all of these "difficult" people to make them the ideal role-model employee? Well, some will never be your role-model employee, but hopefully most of them can be turned around to a positive, involved, and great employee and team player.

Possible Solutions

- For the **Bully/Bullyess** or the **Know-It-All,** you may need to turn the tables on them. Short of a punch in the eye, get their attention and tell them your side. Be friendly and still polite, but stand up for yourself or the team. Allow them time to express their concerns and feelings, but you must inform them of the other concerns of the team or company. Then have them listen to you and explain why another approach could or might work. Take all their suggestions into consideration, listen to any questions or concerns on both sides, but at the end the best person will win.
- The **"Yes" People and Procrastinators** may need more acceptance. These are your employees who want and need more approval, encouragement, and focus. They will need more help in solving challenges, finding a comfort zone, and compromising. Just watch that these employees do not pull other employees into their fold.
- The **Snippy** and **Pessimist** individual may need you to listen more than talk. This group may complain on a regular basis, so your job is just to acknowledge, not necessarily to agree or accept. At times they may shoot from the hip even if they know all the facts and details, and probably with no prior research.
- **Indecisive** employees may actually just clam up. With these folks, you have several options: to terminate the meeting, sit and listen, or encourage them with open-ended questions requiring more than a yes, no, or one-word answer.

- The **Silent** person must be handled delicately and with sensitivity. Perhaps these people don't have the answers, or are just reticient to speak up in front of the group. If they do choose to respond but their answer is not at all correct, thank them and then "wordsmith" their comments so it is indeed the correct response.
- The **"Overly Talkative"** can be both your best friend and worst nightmare. If no one responds to your opening questions, this is the type who already has the answer. On the other hand, don't let it get out of control. Ask that person to help you by writing the group's responses on the flip chart. Sometimes the group will handle these "eager beavers" on their own.
- The **Argumentative** individual could be dangerous. Keep your temper in check but remain in control. If this person makes a clearly incorrect answer, throw it to the group for discussion. If need be, talk to the individual privately at break time.
- For **Ramblers** who talk abut everything except the topic at hand, interrupt them when they take a breath and thank them for their comments, but acknowledge that while their comments are interesting, you are getting off the subject. Note that if time permits, the group can revisit those ideas later on in the day.
- For the **Side Talkers,** call on one of them and ask how they felt about the previous comment just made by one of the group. If you tend to walk around the room, stand beside or behind them and if their side conversation still persists, tell one of them what they're talking about is interesting, but you're not sure everyone else could have heard it, and ask them to repeat it.

Ten Tips That Can Help

There are difficult people everywhere you turn. They are not only at work, but could be a parent on your child's soccer team or someone you encounter driving down the highway and switching lanes constantly with no turn signal, at a concert or sports event, taking your parking spot in the garage, or even disagreeing with you in church. You can't get away from them, and at times all of us can be a little difficult. So how do you handle them and make them a little nicer to work and play with?

1. **Don't cave in.** Don't turn around and act exactly as they are by losing your temper or saying something you will regret later. Stay professional.
2. **Listen instead of speak.** Ask them what the problem is and why they are always so frustrated. They may even answer you and get to the root of their frustration.
3. **Don't rush.** Their problems and style of working could be accumulating over years of frustration and stress and you may never know the bottom line or hidden reasons for their lifestyle and inhibitions. If you are calm with them, it may relax them and move them in the correct direction.
4. **Include them.** A lot of times difficult people at work are also loners. Ask them to come to lunch with you, invite them for a cup of coffee after work, and include them on a committee at work. They may turn you down time after time, but keep trying to include them.
5. **Respect.** Most of the time difficult people do have great ideas and are generally very knowledgeable about their job. They may not see the "big picture" of the company, but respect their input and contributions. Slowly try and work them into the bigger picture and how their knowledge in their department or area could be a tremendous asset to the overall "big picture" and goals of the company.
6. **Tolerate.** Unfortunately this is not a good solution, but it's what happens many times. The person is excellent in completing their work, handling all items properly, and fixing or catching any problems or errors. But the rest of the office has a hard time working with this person or including him or her as part of the team. But this coworker is tolerated because he or she does a good job and follows the procedures of the office.
7. **Involve or assign.** At times difficult employees just need to be involved and a part of the team. Give them a responsibility that they must complete, but with the help and input of others. It could be difficult for all involved but could start a slow process for them feeling a little more involved.

8. **Start small.** Don't try to overcome all of their challenges in one big step. It won't work. Start small with little involvement in group team efforts. If they feel rushed or too much involvement, it could totally backfire and the situation could only get worse.

9. **Handle privately.** Do not approach or address the issues openly or publicly. You, as facilitator or trainer, hopefully will have a huge impact on this person. Choose your words well, be prepared before you meet with this employee, and make sure your tone and body language is not confusing. Discuss the issues, have a plan, and provide various alternatives and numerous actions to reach an agreement.

10. **Higher evaluations.** As a last resort after all else fails, you may need to take this to your human resources department, to your supervisor, or to the head of the company. The level of the person you involve for help depends on the setup and size of your office and company. It is highly recommended that you try to find solutions and ways for this to work before reporting or expressing a need for help to a higher level. Hopefully, a trained human resources staff person may be able to turn or guide your difficult employee into a productive and more involved employee.

The Sometimes Difficult People

We all have seen participants who can be difficult from time to time. These are the ones who don't want to work on certain projects, "pretend" they are sick all the time and miss a lot of work, procrastinate, moan and groan, throw in some snide remarks from time to time about the job or other employees, and just border on the negative edge. These people are easier to help recover and change into a positive employee. You may still need to consider some of the above tips and suggestions, but start the process in the early stages. Do not allow these sometimes difficult people to move into the full-fledged stage as a difficult employee. If you allow these bad habits to continue, it changes the morale of the other employees and can escalate the problems and challenges.

Summary

Don't expect a change in the difficult person to happen instantly, and in some cases it may not happen at all. Give the difficult person various options and hopefully you may see a significant change. Unfortunately, it may result in termination or a change to a different area or position where involvement with other employees is not such a major factor. Changing that person's position may not correct his or her issues, but it will keep the morale of your other employees at least stable.

Take This Job

- To take a serious look at some of the negative parts of our job and some of the difficult people with whom we work

Materials

Watch or stopwatch

Time

10 to 15 minutes

Procedure

Suggest that in today's society, workplace violence is an all-too-common occurrence. Tell the group to form into teams of three or four and ask them to confide in one another some things about their jobs or coworkers that tend to have a negative effect on others. (If some feel hesitant to say anything, ask them to think about a past job or situation that was less than productive or harmonious.)

Allow five minutes for this and then ask if anyone would care to tell the whole group about their job or colleague, either past or present. It might be advisable to suggest that "what happens in Vegas . . ." If discussion is waning, have a few situations or scenarios you've either read or heard about and discuss those.

Discussion Questions

1. Why is workplace violence so common today?

2. How many of you recalled a situation from the past that actually caused you to leave that particular job?

3. Why do you suppose some people get their "kicks" from ruining someone else's day?

4. What are some suggestions you can offer to bring about more harmonious work situations?

Connecting to People—Even the Difficult Ones!

Materials

Items that attendees bring that show their passion in life

Time

At least 5 minutes for setup, then 1 minute per person

Procedure

Note: This activity needs to be announced in advance so attendees are able to bring their "show and tell" items.

Even difficult coworkers and employees have a passion. In this activity, you will allow all attendees to display their passion. In advance, advise the attendees to bring either the item or a picture of the item that provides them passion. This could be a picture of their family, an instrument they love to play, a cake because they love to bake wedding or themed cakes, and so on. This could be a process to bring out the best in all people and also an opportunity to share their feelings. Many times a difficult employee just needs to be involved and a part of the team. They may even "shock" their coworkers or fellow attendees by showing this other side to them. This is an excellent opportunity to start bringing the team together and breaking down barriers.

Discussion Questions

1. Were you surprised by anyone's passion?

2. Do you live this passion or only hope or dream it?

3. If you only hope or dream, what will help you get there?

Brain Teaser #7

Directions

Decipher the hidden meaning of each box. See page ix for additional instructions.

1.	2.	3.	4.
CHATTE	UTA	appolis	1,000,1000
5. ⊘ CHANCE	6.　I 　I 　V	7.　　the 　　market	8.　SA SA stories
9.	10.　U　　　　P	11.　NIINTE	12.　**BERRY**
13.　AGOODL 　GUY 　L	14.　erutuf2	15.　　L 　　A 　　I 　　D 　Internet	16.　Jack

Brain Teaser #7 Answers

1. Endless chatter

2. Back at you

3. Minneapolis

4. One in a million

5. Not a chance

6. Seven-Up

7. Corner the market

8. Essays and short stories

9. Theatre in the round

10. Split up

11. In the middle of the nite

12. BlackBerry

13. All-around good guy

14. Back to the future

15. Dial-up Internet

16. Jack in the box

About the Authors

Colleen A. Rickenbacher, CMP, CSEP, CPC, CTA, is a business owner, etiquette and protocol consultant, author, speaker, and trainer. Speaking engagements on the importance of protocol and etiquette in your professional and personal life have taken Colleen around the world. She can be seen and heard regularly on national television and radio including Country Music Television with the Dallas Cowboys Cheerleaders, Fox News, and various other programs.

Colleen was recognized by *MeetingNews* magazine as one of the Top 25 Most Influential People in the Meetings Industry. Most recently she was inducted into the Hall of Fame and awarded the Lifetime Achievement designation by *Texas Meetings & Events* magazine, which is their highest honor.

Her book *Be on Your Best Business Behavior* covers all areas of practical business and dining skills. The tips she provides will strengthen your image and that of your organization. It is never too early or too late to learn skills that will separate you from your competition.

Her book, *Be on Your Best Cultural Behavior,* covers the proper etiquette and protocol in 33 countries. These guidelines will allow you to navigate globally in our international climate whether you do business in other countries or never leave your backyard.

Colleen's speaking engagements are extensive and she has been featured in numerous meeting industry publications.

Colleen achieved her Certified Meeting Professional (CMP) in 1992, the Certified Special Events Professional (CSEP) in 2001, her Certified Protocol Consultant (CPC) in 2006, and, most recently, her Certified Tourism Ambassador (CTA) in 2010.

She presently serves on the Meeting Professionals International (MPI) Foundation's Board of Trustees and previously served on the MPI Board of Directors as Board Liaison for the Chancellors and also as Past President of the Dallas/Fort Worth Chapter. Other boards have included the Certified Meeting Professional Board (as Chair), Association of Event and Convention Professionals (TxACOM) (as the First President), the Charter Board of Directors of the Dallas Chapter of the International Special Events Society (ISES), and the Board of Directors for the International Special Events Society.

Edward E. Scannell, CMP, CSP, is an active member of the National Speakers Association and has given more than a thousand presentations, seminars, and workshops across the United States and in several overseas venues.

He has written or coauthored more than 20 books and over a hundred articles in the fields of HRD, creativity, team building, and management. His *Games Trainers Play* series has sold over a million copies throughout the world.

Ed has served as the National President of the American Society for Training and Development (ASTD) and also as Executive Chairman for the International Federation of Training and Development Organizations (IFTDO).

A past President of the Arizona Chapter of Meeting Professionals International (MPI), he was elected as MPI's International President in 1990–91. He served as Chair of MPI's Chancellors and also as Dean of the MPI Institute Program. He was named MPI's International Planner of the Year in 1995 and was one of only five individuals inducted into the Convention Industry Hall of Leaders in 2007.

Ed was elected National President of the National Speakers Association (NSA) in 1991–92 and received NSA's highest honor, the Cavett Award, in 1999.

He taught at both the University of Northern Iowa and Arizona State University's College of Business.

He is currently serving as the Director of the Center for Professional Development and Training in Scottsdale, Arizona.